Ninja Foodi Dual Air Fryer Cookbook UK

These Delicious and Easy Air Fryer Recipes Will Satisfy Your Everyday and Festive Cooking Needs

Amelie Myers

© **Copyright 2022 - All Rights Reserved**

Under no circumstances, no part of this publication may be reproduced, distributed, or transmitted in any form or by any means, including photocopying, recording, or other electronic or mechanical methods, or by any information storage and retrieval system without the prior written permission of the copyright holder.

The information in this book is accurate and complete; however, the author and the publisher do not warrant the accuracy of the information, text, and graphics contained within the book due to the rapidly changing nature of science, research, known and unknown facts, and internet. The author and the publisher do not hold any responsibility for errors, omissions, or contrary interpretation of the subject matter herein. This book is presented solely for motivational and informational purposes only.

Contents

1   **Introduction**

2   **Fundamentals of Ninja Foodi 2-Basket Air Fryer**

What is Ninja Foodi 2-Basket Air Fryer 2
Benefits of Using it 2
Step-By-Step Guide of Using Ninja Foodi 2-Basket Air Fryer 3
Cooking in Your 2-Basket Air Fryer 4
Tips for Accessories 5
Cleaning and Caring Ninja Foodi 2-Basket Air Fryer 6
Frequently Asked Questions and Notes   6

8   **4-Week Diet Plan**

Week 1.................... 8
Week 2.................... 8
Week 3.................... 9
Week 4.................... 9

10   **Chapter 1 Breakfast Recipes**

Cinnamon Butter Toast 10
Simple Baked Bagels 10
Sweet Bacon Cinnamon Rolls 11
Vanilla Cinnamon Rolls 11
Banana Bread with Walnuts 12
Raspberry Puff Pastry 12
Cinnamon French Toast Sticks 13
Egg in a Hole 13
Avocado Egg Cups 14
Air Fryer Apples with Cinnamon Oats   14
Cream Bacon & Spinach Cups 15
Spicy Breakfast Potatoes.................. 15
Salmon Onion Quiche.................... 16
Sesame Yoghurt Bagels 16
Sausage & Bacon Omelet with Onion   17
Savory Peppers Soufflé 17
Baked Parmesan Eggs.................... 18
Homemade French Toasts 18
Banana Blueberry Muffins 19
Simple Hard Boiled Eggs 19
Cheese Mushroom Rolls................. 20
Spicy Beef Skewers 20

20   **Chapter 2 Snack and Starter Recipes**

Spicy Pumpkin Fries 21

Contents | 03

Garlic Butter Bread 21	Cheesy Bacon Stuffed Mushrooms 33
Beef Mushroom Pastry 22	Baked Garlicky Mushrooms 34
Cheese Turkey Croquettes 22	Buttery Squash slices 34
Crispy Breaded Calamari Rings 23	Healthy Beans & Veggie Burgers 35
Cheese Spinach Patties 23	Chili Butternut Squash 35
Breaded Mozzarella Sticks 24	Crispy Herb Potatoes 36
Easy Potato Fries........................... 24	Crispy Courgette Fries 36
Homemade Soft Pretzels.................. 25	Vegetable Stuffed Peppers 37
Easy Pretzels Dogs 25	Crispy Cheese Garlic Broccoli 37
Air Fryer Cheese Chicken Wings 26	Air Fryer Rice with Peas & Carrots ... 38
Cheese Beef Taquitos 26	Tofu in Ginger Orange Sauce........... 38
Crispy Fried Okra 27	Spicy Buttered Cauliflower............... 39
Potato Waffle Fries 27	Simple Buttered Green Beans........... 39
Cumin Potato Tacos 28	Honey Glazed Carrots..................... 40
Crispy Avocado Fries 28	Classic Hasselback Potatoes 40
Spicy Cauliflower Poppers 29	Spiced Butter Courgette 41
Fresh Kale Chips 29	Easy Balsamic Asparagus 41
Cheese & Brown Rice Stuffed Tomatoes 30	Cheese Crumb-Topped Sole 42
Spicy Fried Green Tomatoes 30	Cheese Prawn Salad 42

30 Chapter 3 Vegetable and Sides Recipes

42 Chapter 4 Fish and Seafood Recipes

Avocado Tacos with Veggie 31	Coconut Prawns in Buns.................. 43
Baked Balsamic Brussel Sprouts 31	Prawns in Tacos with Coleslaw 43
Air Fryer Red Potato Bites 32	Crispy Oysters............................... 44
Garlic Cheese Asparagus 32	Honey Glazed Tuna Steaks 44
Crispy Cheese Aubergine 33	Cheese-Crusted Tuna Patties 45

Garlicky Teriyaki Salmon 45	Spiced Chicken Wings 58
Salmon Cakes with Mayonnaise 46	Buttered Chicken Breast 58
Korean-Style Prawn Skewers 46	Cheese Chicken Pockets 59
Sweet Fried Salmon 47	Delicious Chicken Pesto Stuffed Peppers 59
Air Fried Salmon Fillets 47	Fried Chicken with Cheese and Pasta Sauce 60
Delicious Cod Cakes 48	Air Fried Curry Chicken Drumsticks ... 60
Lemony Salmon 48	Cheese Onion & Green Peppers Stuffed Chicken 61
Sweet and Spicy Salmon 49	Crispy Almond Chicken 61
Air Fryer Salmon with Asparagus 49	Herbed Fried Chicken 62
Lemon Garlic Tilapia 50	Sweet Potato-Crusted Chicken 62
Tasty Breaded Tilapia 50	Bagel Crusted Chicken Strips 63
Spicy Cajun Cod Fillets 51	Lemony Cheese Chicken 63
Crispy and Spicy Catfish.................. 51	Hot and Spicy Chicken 64
Garlic Butter Prawns with Parsley 52	Spicy Roasted Whole Chicken 64
Simple Fried Salmon 52	Sour and Spicy Chicken Legs 65
Spicy Salmon with Lemon 53	Paprika Chicken Legs 65
Spicy Fried Scallops 53	Honey & Mustard Glazed Chicken Drumsticks 66
Sweet & Sour Salmon 54	Gingered Coconut Chicken Drumsticks 66
Herbed Salmon with Asparagus 54	Smoked Spicy Chicken Thighs 67
Chicken & Rice Stuffed Peppers 55	Buttered Chicken Thighs 67
Spiced Duck Legs 55	Crispy Chicken Breasts with Coriander 68

55 Chapter 5 Poultry Mains Recipes

Beer-Braised Duck Breast 56	Parmesan Chicken Breasts with Basil 68
Herbed Lime Gingered Turkey Legs ... 56	Cheese Chicken Cordon Bleu............ 69
Homemade Chicken Tenders 57	
Breaded Chicken Cutlets.................. 57	

Cheese & Spinach Stuffed Chicken ... 69
Rosemary Lime Turkey Legs 70
Simple Baked Turkey Breast 70
Garlicky Herbed Duck Legs 71
Easy Lamb Steak 72
Simple Beef Roast 72

72 Chapter 6 Beef, Pork & Lamb Recipes

Bacon Wrapped Filet Mignon 73
Delicious BBQ Pork Loin 73
Sweet BBQ Pork Ribs.................... 74
Air Fried New York Strip Steak 74
Bacon Wrapped Hot Dogs 75
Seasoned Steak 75
Herbed Pork Chops...................... 76
Garlicky Lamb Loin Chops 76
Cinnamon Lamb Meatballs............... 77
Delicious Cajun Flank Steak 77
Herbed Lamb Chops 78
Easy Baked Lamb Steaks 78
Herbed Beef Roast 79
BBQ Baby Back Ribs 79
Baked Pork Chops with Herbs 80
Pork Tenderloin 80
Bacon Wrapped Pork Tenderloin 81
Simple Seasoned Lamb Chops 81

Oreo Muffins 82
Lemony Cheesecake 82

82 Chapter 7 Dessert Recipes

Oatmeal Butter Cookies 83
Chocolate Cake 83
Mini Apple Pies 84
Homemade Churros 84
Dough Dippers with Chocolate Amaretto Sauce 85
Raisin and Almond Stuffed Apples...... 85
Air Fryer Butter Brownies 86
Baked Citrus Mousse 86
Cheese Apple Pie Rolls 87
Traditional Chocolate Muffins 87
Delicious Vanilla Soufflé 88
Easy Chocolate Mug Cakes 88
Fresh Blueberry Cobbler.................. 89
Buttered Cherry Crumble 89
Plum and Oats Cup 90

91 Conclusion

92 Appendix 1 Air Fryer Cooking Chart

93 Appendix 2 Recipes Index

Introduction

One of the rare air fryers having two cooking zones with a combined capacity of 10 quarts is the Ninja Foodi 2-Basket Air Fryer. It is a multifunctional kitchen tool that can air fry, broil, roast, bake, dehydrate, and reheat leftovers. The Ninja Double Air Fryer also comes with useful smart features. With a double-basket configuration, it boasts the largest cooking capacity. The Ninja Foodi 6-in-1 10-quart 2-Basket Air Fryer is a powerful device with multiple baskets to help you get the most out of air frying. It provides additional room for air-frying huge quantities of food and permits the simultaneous cooking of two separate dishes.

This appliance swiftly prepares nutritious meals and makes cleanup simple. In addition to the vast real estate cooking, it has a few clever features. The traditional single-basket air fryer has been replaced with the first air fryer with two independent baskets. One thing to keep in mind is that using both baskets result in lengthier cooking times for both than doing so with just one basket.

Fundamentals of Ninja Foodi 2-Basket Air Fryer

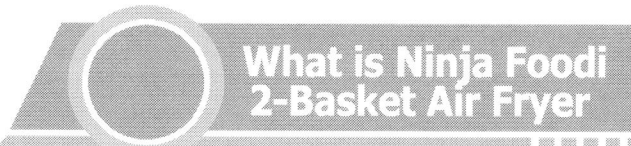

What is Ninja Foodi 2-Basket Air Fryer

The first air fryer with two separate baskets that allows you to cook two items at once is the Ninja Foodi 2-Basket Air Fryer with Dual Zone Technology. Not parallel to each other like in a conventional single-basket air fryer. The Smart Finish function of Dual Zone Technology cleverly coordinates cooking so that both items are finished at the same time. The fact that it can be programmed is its most unique feature. It is a grey object with the following measurements: 13.86"D x 15.63"W x 12.4"H. It has a 10-quart capacity divided between two 5-quart baskets. It is constructed of plastic. It is advised to use it for roasting, broiling, baking, reheating, as well as dehydrating.

Benefits of Using it

Improved Cooking. The likelihood of healthier cooking is the single most significant factor for the majority of people purchasing an air fryer.

Fast, Safe, and Easy to Use

Crisp & Crunchy Food

It's Very Versatile

Faster Than Oven Cooking

Reheat Foods with Ease

Easy to Clean

From being novel and inventive, air fryers are now widely used. But it doesn't imply there isn't any fresh information available. The lack of room issue is resolved by the Ninja model, and chefs are no longer forced to decide whether to air fry the wings or the fries. Because of the two baskets and the independent controls for the left and right sides, each side may have its own time and temperature settings. But the Smart Finish and Match choices are much better.

With Smart Finish, the cook may select distinct cooking durations and temperatures for each basket and then delegate commencing the shorter cooking period to the appliance, resulting in the completion of the two things at the same time. Naturally, this is useless if the cook is estimating the length of time something will take to prepare, but it works well when cooking family favourites like fish and chips, which are prepared simultaneously.

The settings are simply repeated from one side to the other when using the Match option. It's hardly a revolutionary invention, but it's convenient to be able to set the time and temperature once, and start both at the same time, while a double batch of wings is in the fryer. Ninja also states that it uses 75% less energy than a standard oven.

Step-By-Step Guide of Using Ninja Foodi 2-Basket Air Fryer

Function Buttons

Air Broil: Give dishes a crispy finishing touch or melt toppings for the ideal presentation.

Air Fry: Use the air fryer to add crunch and crispness to your cuisine while using little to no oil.

Roast: Use the appliance as a roaster oven for a variety of foods.

Reheat: Warm up your leftovers so they come out crispy.

Dehydrate: Dehydrate fruits, vegetables, and meats for wholesome snacking.

Bake: Make opulent sweets and baked goods.

Operating Buttons

Button "1": Regulates the basket's output on the left.

Button "2": Regulates the output for the right-hand basket.

TEMP arrows: To change the cook temperature before or while cooking, use the up and down arrows.

TIME arrows: To change the cook time in any function before or during the cook cycle, use the up and down arrows.

Air Fry

1. Place the crisper plate in the basket, add the contents, and then put the basket into the appliance.
2. The device will automatically enter zone 1 (to use zone 2 instead, select zone 2). Choose AIR FRY.
3. To choose the preferred temperature, use the TEMP arrows.
4. To set the time in 1-minute increments up to an hour, use the TIME arrows. To start cooking, press the START/PAUSE button.
5. The appliance will beep and "End" will show up on the display when cooking is finished.
6. Utilize tongs or tools with a silicone tip to remove the ingredients.

Bake

1. Place the crisper plate in the basket, add the contents, and then put the basket into the appliance.
2. The device will automatically enter zone 1 (to use zone 2 instead, select zone 2). Choose Bake.
3. To choose the preferred temperature, use the TEMP arrows.
4. To set the time in 1-minute increments up to an hour, and time in 5-minute increments from 1 to 4 hours use the TIME arrows. To start cooking. Press the START/PAUSE button to begin cooking.
5. The appliance will beep and "End" will show up on the display when cooking is finished.
6. Utilize tongs or tools with a silicone tip to remove the ingredients.

Roast

1. Place items in the basket, add a crisper plate if desired, and then put the basket into the appliance.
2. The device will automatically enter zone 1 (to use zone 2 instead, select zone 2). Choose ROAST.
3. To choose the preferred temperature, use the TEMP arrows.
4. To set the time in 1-minute increments up to an hour and in 5-minute increments from an hour to four hours, use the TIME arrows. To start cooking, press the START/PAUSE button.
5. The appliance will beep and "End" will show up on the display when cooking is finished.
6. Utilize tongs or tools with a silicone tip to remove the ingredients.

Reheat

1. Place the crisper plate in the basket, add the contents, and then put the basket into the appliance.
2. The device will automatically enter zone 1 (to use zone 2

instead, select zone 2). Choose Reheat.

3. To choose the preferred temperature, use the TEMP arrows.

4. To set the time in 1-minute increments up to an hour, use the TIME arrows. To start reheating, press the START/PAUSE button.

5. The appliance will beep and "End" will show up on the display when cooking is finished.

6. Utilize tongs or tools with a silicone tip to remove the ingredients.

Dehydrate

1. Arrange the ingredients in a single layer in the basket. Then, after placing the crisper plate in the basket on top of the first layer, add a second layer of ingredients.

2. The gadget will by default be in zone 1. (Choose zone 2 to utilize it in its place.) Decide on DEHYDRATE. By default, the display will show the temperature as it is. Use the TEMP arrows to select your ideal temperature.

3. Use the TIME arrows to set the time in 15-minute intervals between 1 and 12 hours. To begin the dehydration process, use the START/PAUSE button.

4. When cooking is complete, the appliance will beep and the word "End" will appear on the display.

5. Utilize tongs or tools with a silicone tip to remove the ingredients.

Air Broil

1. Place the crisper plate in the basket, add the contents, and then put the basket into the appliance.

2. The device will automatically enter zone 1 (to use zone 2 instead, select zone 2). Choose AIR BROIL.

3. To choose the preferred temperature, use the TEMP arrows.

4 | Fundamentals of Ninja Foodi 2-Basket Air Fryer

4. To set the time in 1-minute increments up to 30 minutes, use the TIME arrows. To start cooking, press the START/PAUSE button.

5. The appliance will beep and "End" will show up on the display when cooking is finished.

6. Utilize tongs or tools with a silicone tip to remove the ingredients.

Two cooking zones are used in Dual Zone Technology to maximise flexibility. Regardless of the cook settings, the Smart Finish function guarantees that both zones will be finished and ready to serve at the same time.

Smart Finish

When meals have varied cook times, temperatures, or even functions, to finish cooking at the same time:

1. Fill the baskets with materials, then put the baskets inside the apparatus.

2. Zone 1 will continue to be lit up. Choose the cooking option that you want. Set the temperature using the TEMP arrows, and the time with the TIME arrows.

3. Choose the required cooking function after choosing zone 2. (If zone 1 is chosen, AIR BROIL is not an option.) Set the temperature using the TEMP arrows, and the time with the TIME arrows.

4. To start cooking in the zone with the longest cooking time, press SMART FINISH, then push the START/PAUSE button. Hold will be seen in the opposite zone. When both zones have the same amount of time left, the unit will beep and activate the second zone.

5. The appliance will beep and "End" will show up on the display when cooking is finished.

6. Utilize tongs or tools with a silicone tip to remove the ingredients. DON'T put a drawer on top of the appliance.

Match Cook

To cook various meals at the same function, temperature, and time while cooking more of the same food:

1. Fill the baskets with materials, then put the baskets inside the apparatus.

2. Zone 1 will continue to be lit up. Choose the cooking option that you want. (This function does not include AIR BROIL.) Set the temperature using the TEMP arrows, and the time with the TIME arrows.

3. Push the MATCH COOK button to transfer the settings from zone 1 to zone 2. After that, press START/PAUSE to start the stoves in both zones.

4. When cooking stops simultaneously on both screens, the word "End" will appear.

5. Utilize tongs or tools with a silicone tip to remove the ingredients.

Starting Both Zones at the Same Time, but Ending at Different Times

1. Zone 1 should be chosen before the required function. To adjust the temperature, use the TEMP arrows.

2. To set the time, use the TIME arrows.

3. For zone 2, repeat steps 2 and 3. (If set to zone 1, AIR BROIL is not accessible.)

4. To start the cooking process in both zones, press the START/PAUSE button.

5. The appliance will beep and "End" will show up on the display after cooking has finished in each zone.

6. Remove the ingredients by emptying them out or removing them with tongs or tools that have silicone tips.

Ending the Cook Time in One Zone (While Using Both Zones)

1. Pick the area where you want to stop.

2. To reset the time to zero, push the down arrow on the TIME button.

3. Press the START/PAUSE button once you have reset the time to zero.

4. After that, the time in that zone is cancelled, and the word "End" will show up on the display. The other area will still be used

Pausing Both Zones at the Same Time

1. Press the START/PAUSE button to pause time in the SMART FINISH mode or to pause both zones in dual zone cooking.

2. Press the START/PAUSE button once again to resume cooking.

Pausing a Single Zone During Dual Zone Cooking

1. Select the zone you wish to halt time in, then hit the START/PAUSE button while both zones are still active.

2. Press the START/PAUSE button once more to start cooking again.

Cooking in a Single Zone

Plug the power cable into a wall socket, then push the power button to turn the device on.

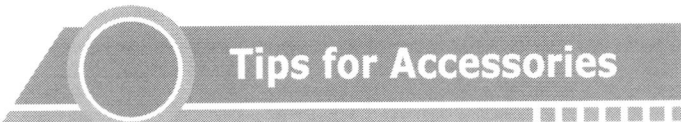

Tips for Accessories

Here are a few of my recommendations after you know what Ninja Foodi accessories you require and are prepared to go purchasing. There are so many alternatives available that it can be challenging to choose which attachments will function the best, suit the Ninja Foodi, and last.

For any of the Tender Crisp lid functions and steaming, oven-safe (up to 425°F) glass is OK, however, pressure cooking may not be possible. When pressure cooking, always use glass or porcelain that is pressure-rated; otherwise, you run the danger of it breaking under pressure, which would undoubtedly spoil supper.

If it fits within the Ninja Foodi, any aluminium or metal pan may be used with all of the Ninja Foodi's features.

With all of the features, silicone goods may be used in the Ninja Foodi without issue, but you should be aware that it does not transfer heat as well as other materials. This indicates that you should definitely extend the cooking time if you are using silicone in a recipe that asks for a glass or metal baking dish.

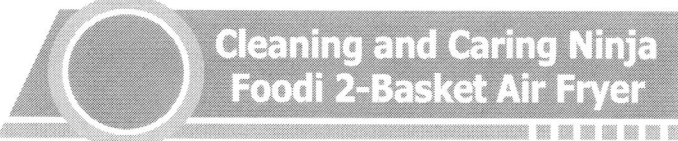

Cleaning and Caring Ninja Foodi 2-Basket Air Fryer

Cleaning up is simple as pie. The basket and crisper plate may simply be loaded into the dishwasher because it is dishwasher safe. If not, you may always wash it by hand, which is equally simple.

The majority of food residue will easily come off because of the non-stick coating. By the way, to avoid harming the coating, just use a soft sponge and non-abrasive cleaning. Last but not least, clean the main unit with a moist cloth.

Main Unit: Use a moist cloth to clean the main unit and the control panel. NEVER submerge the main unit in water or any other liquid, it should be noted. NEVER clean a dishwasher's main unit.

Crisper Plates: You may either hand-wash or put your crisper plates in the dishwasher. After using, air-dry or towel-dry all portions if you washed them by hand.

Baskets: You may hand-wash or put them in the dishwasher to clean. After usage, air-dry or towel-dry all components if hand-washing. To increase the lifespan of your basket, we advise hand-washing them.

Frequently Asked Questions and Notes

Q) How can I change the time or the temperature when utilizing a single zone?

By using the up/down arrows while a single zone is operating, the time or temperature may be changed whenever you choose.

Q) How can I change the time or the temperature while utilizing both zones?

Use the TEMP arrows to change the temperature or the TIME arrows to change the time after choosing the desired zone.

Q) Can I prepare various dishes without worrying about cross-contamination in each zone?

Yes, each zones have independent heating elements and fans and are self-contained.

Q) When using both zones, how can I pause or stop one?

Press the START/PAUSE button after choosing the zone you want to pause or stop.

Q) Can I safely place the baskets on my countertop?

During cooking, the baskets will warm up. Handle them carefully, and only put them on surfaces that can withstand heat. The baskets SHOULD NOT be positioned on the unit's top.

Q) In What circumstances should I utilize the crisper plate?

Whenever you want your meal to be crisp, use the crisper plate. The plate raises the contents of the basket so that air can circulate beneath and around it, evenly cooking the food.

Q) Why didn't my meal finish cooking?

During cooking, make sure the basket is fully inserted. Make sure the ingredients are layered evenly and without overlap on the bottom of the basket for uniform browning. Toss ingredients with a shake to ensure uniform crispness. You may alter the cooking temperature and duration at any moment. Simply use the TEMP arrows or the TIME arrows to change the temperature or the time.

Q) My meal is scorched, why?

For the best results, keep an eye on the food while it cooks and remove it when the ideal amount of brownness is reached. To prevent overcooking, remove food from the oven as soon as the cooking time is over.

Q) When air frying, why do some components flutter about?

On occasion, the air fryer's fan will fling light meals in all directions. To hold loose, light food, such as the top piece of bread on a sandwich, in place, use wooden toothpicks.

Q) Can I cook wet, battered ingredients in the air?

Yes, but be sure you bread your food properly. It's crucial to cover meals with flour, egg, and then bread crumbs in that order. To prevent crumbs from being blown off by the fan, press the breading firmly into the battered items.

Q) What caused the screen to go black?

The device is set to standby. To restart it, press the power button.

Q) Why does the device beep?

The dish has either finished cooking or the other zone has begun.

Q) What caused a circuit breaker to trip while the device was in use?

The device has to be plugged into an outlet with a 15-amp circuit breaker since it consumes 1690 watts of electricity. A 10-amp breaker will trip if an outlet is used while it is on. The device must also be the only appliance connected to an outlet while it is in operation. Make sure the appliance is the only one connected to an outlet on a 15-amp breaker to prevent tripping the breaker.

Notes

You may take the basket out during cooking to shake or toss the contents for evening crisping. During this period, you can pause by pressing the zone number followed by START/PAUSE. Press START/PAUSE if just one zone is being used.

You can STOP A ZONE if you determine that the food in one of the zones is finished cooking before the allotted cook time has passed. Press START/PAUSE or set the time to 0 to pause cooking after selecting that

4-Week Diet Plan

Week 1

Day 1:
Breakfast: Butter Bread
Lunch: Buttered Peas
Snack: Homemade Sausage Rolls
Dinner: Golden Cajun Fish Fillets
Dessert: Easy Apple Crumble

Day 2:
Breakfast: Traditional Scottish Porridge
Lunch: Cheese Cauliflower
Snack: Prawns with Spicy Sauce
Dinner: Honey Roast Duck with Thyme
Dessert: Quick and Easy Banoffee Pie

Day 3:
Breakfast: Homemade Crumpets
Lunch: Thyme Parsnip Soup
Snack: Creamy Leek & Potato Soup with Bread
Dinner: Cheese Turkey Ciabatta
Dessert: Bread and Raisin Pudding

Day 4:
Breakfast: Traditional English Breakfast
Lunch: Traditional Rumbled Thumps
Snack: Yellow Split Pea Ham Soup
Dinner: Simple Fish Fillets
Dessert: Cherry Tart

Day 5:
Breakfast: Grilled Haddock
Lunch: Cheese Leek Sausages
Snack: Classic Welsh Rarebit
Dinner: Easy Fried Duck Breast
Dessert: Classic Yorkshire Curd Tart

Day 6:
Breakfast: Tasty Potato Scone
Lunch: Tasty Scottish Stovies
Snack: Bacon-Wrapped Chicken
Dinner: Herb Roast Beef
Dessert: Lemon Spotted Dick

Day 7:
Breakfast: Potato Bread Farls
Lunch: Vegan Shepherd's Pie
Snack: Easy Yorkshire Pudding
Dinner: Buttered Herb Turkey Breast
Dessert: Homemade Welsh Cakes

Week 2

Day 1:
Breakfast: Apple Ravioli
Lunch: Cheese and Leek tart
Snack: Traditional Bubble and Squeak
Dinner: Crispy Potato-Crusted Fish
Dessert: Apple Cake

Day 2:
Breakfast: Easy Soda Bread
Lunch: Cheese Fennel and Mushrooms Tartlets
Snack: Scottish Cullen Skink
Dinner: Herb-Roasted Lamb
Dessert: Scottish Dundee Cake

Day 3:
Breakfast: Rice with Eggs and Tofu
Lunch: Thyme Pumpkin Soup
Snack: Air fryer Sausage and Chips
Dinner: Turkey Strips with Three Peppers
Dessert: Easy Peach Cobbler

Day 4:
Breakfast: Scottish Short Bread Cookies
Lunch: All-Vegetable Toad in The Hole
Snack: Delicious Beef Wellington Bites
Dinner: Simple Air Fryer Sausages
Dessert: Rhubarb Muffins with Oats Crumble

Day 5:
Breakfast: Simple Poached Eggs on Toast
Lunch: Pea and Mint Soup with Ham
Snack: Mushroom and Prosciutto on Toast
Dinner: Pork Cassoulet with Beans and Carrots
Dessert: Victoria Sponge Cake

Day 6:
Breakfast: Classic Eggs Benedict
Lunch: Cheese Potato & Lentil Pie
Snack: Potted Prawns with Bread
Dinner: Spicy Turkey Wings
Dessert: Baked Manchester Tart

Day 7:
Breakfast: Scrambled Eggs with Smoked Salmon
Lunch: Herby Veggie Balls
Snack: Pineapple Sticks with Yogurt Dip
Dinner: Beer Battered Cod
Dessert: Oat Flapjacks

Week 3

Day 1:
Breakfast: Hot Cross Buns
Lunch: Vegetarian Cheese Bean Patties
Snack: Air fry Brussels Sprouts with Bacon
Dinner: Herbed Turkey Crown
Dessert: Custard Tart with Nutmeg

Day 2:
Breakfast: Tuscan Bean Tomato Toast
Lunch: Roasted Potatoes
Snack: Air fryer Sausage and Chips
Dinner: Spicy Lemon Fish
Dessert: Apple Cake with Walnut

Day 3:
Breakfast: Strawberry Jam On toast
Lunch: Cheese Cauliflower
Snack: Crispy Fish and Chips
Dinner: Air Fryer Garlic Prawns
Dessert: Simple Apple Pie

Day 4:
Breakfast: Baked Eggs and Salmon
Lunch: Buttered Peas
Snack: Cockle Pie
Dinner: Roast Lamb Legs with Potatoes
Dessert: Homemade Sweet Potato Pie

Day 5:
Breakfast: Bacon Butty Sandwich
Lunch: Thyme Parsnip Soup
Snack: Grilled Leeks in Cheese Milk Sauce
Dinner: Spicy Turkey Tenderloin
Dessert: Mini Cinnamon Apple Pie

Day 6:
Breakfast: Almond Tarts with Cherry Jam
Lunch: Traditional Rumbled Thumps
Snack: Fish Cakes
Dinner: Air Fryer Beef Hamburgers
Dessert: Easy Apple Crumble

Day 7:
Breakfast: Rhubarb, Pear and Hazelnut Crumble
Lunch: Cheese Leek Sausages
Snack: Delicious Beef Wellington Bites
Dinner: Finnan Haddie
Dessert: Quick and Easy Banoffee Pie

Week 4

Day 1:
Breakfast: Butter Bread
Lunch: Tasty Scottish Stovies
Snack: Halloumi Corn Bites
Dinner: Breaded Chicken Breast
Dessert: Bread and Raisin Pudding

Day 2:
Breakfast: Traditional Scottish Porridge
Lunch: Vegan Shepherd's Pie
Snack: Golden Beef Pies
Dinner: Potted Butter Scallops
Dessert: Cherry Tart

Day 3:
Breakfast: Homemade Crumpets
Lunch: Cheese and Leek tart
Snack: Homemade Sausage Rolls
Dinner: Easy Fried Chicken Legs
Dessert: Classic Yorkshire Curd Tart

Day 4:
Breakfast: Traditional English Breakfast
Lunch: Cheese Fennel and Mushrooms Tartlets
Snack: Prawns with Spicy Sauce
Dinner: Beef, Vegetables with Noodles
Dessert: Lemon Spotted Dick

Day 5:
Breakfast: Grilled Haddock
Lunch: Thyme Pumpkin Soup
Snack: Creamy Leek & Potato Soup with Bread
Dinner: Easy Roast Steak
Dessert: Homemade Welsh Cakes

Day 6:
Breakfast: Tasty Potato Scone
Lunch: All-Vegetable Toad in The Hole
Snack: Yellow Split Pea Ham Soup
Dinner: Italian Seasoned Chicken
Dessert: Apple Cake

Day 7:
Breakfast: Potato Bread Farl
Lunch: Pea and Mint Soup with Ham
Snack: Classic Welsh Rarebit
Dinner: Bacon-Wrapped Oyster
Dessert: Scottish Dundee Cake

Chapter 1 Breakfast Recipes

Cinnamon Butter Toast

Preparation Time: 10 minutes | Cooking Time: 5 minutes | Servings: 6

Ingredients:

- 12 slices bread
- 115g butter, at room temperature
- 100g white sugar
- 1½ teaspoons ground cinnamon
- 1½ teaspoons pure vanilla extract
- 1 pinch of salt

Preparation:

1. Softened butter is mashed with a fork or the back of a spoon, and then sugar, cinnamon, vanilla, and salt are added.
2. Stir everything together thoroughly.
3. Spread one-sixth of the mixture onto each slice of bread, covering the entire surface.
4. Press your chosen zone - "Zone 1" or "Zone 2" and then rotate the knob to select "Air Fryer".
5. Set the temperature to 200 degrees C, and then set the time for 3 minutes to preheat.
6. After preheating, arrange bread into the basket of each zone.
7. Slide the basket into the Air Fryer and set the time for 5 minutes.
8. After cooking time is completed, remove both baskets from Air Fryer.
9. Cut bread slices diagonally and serve.

Serving Suggestions: Serve with maple syrup.
Variation Tip: You can add 2 pinches of black pepper.
Nutritional Information per Serving:
Calories: 355 | Fat: 17g | Sat Fat: 10g | Carbohydrates: 45g | Fibre: 3g | Sugar: 20g | Protein: 6g

Simple Baked Bagels

Preparation Time: 10 minutes | Cooking Time: 15 minutes | Servings: 4

Ingredients:

- 125g self-rising flour
- 240g non-fat plain Greek yoghurt
- 1 beaten egg
- 30g sesame seeds

Preparation:

1. Combine the self-rising flour and Greek yoghurt in a medium mixing bowl using a wooden spoon.
2. Knead the dough for about 5 minutes on a lightly floured board.
3. Divide the dough into four equal pieces. Roll each piece into a thin rope, securing the ends to form a bagel shape. Sprinkle the sesame seeds on it.
4. Press either "Zone 1" or "Zone 2" and then rotate the knob to select "Air Fryer".
5. Set the temperature to 140 degrees C, and then set the time for 3 minutes to preheat.
6. After preheating, arrange bagels into the basket.
7. Slide basket into Air Fryer and set the time for 15 minutes.
8. After cooking time is completed, remove both pans from Air Fryer.
9. Place the bagels onto a wire rack to cool for about 10 minutes and serve.

Serving Suggestions: Serve with avocado.
Variation Tip: You can skip egg wash.
Nutritional Information per Serving:
Calories: 148 | Fat: 1g | Sat Fat: 1g | Carbohydrates: 25g | Fibre: 1g | Sugar: 2g | Protein: 10g

Sweet Bacon Cinnamon Rolls

Preparation Time: 20 minutes | Cooking Time: 10 minutes | Servings: 8

Ingredients:

- 8 bacon strips
- 180ml bourbon
- 1 tube (310g) refrigerated cinnamon rolls with icing
- 55g chopped pecans
- 2 tablespoons maple syrup

Preparation:

1. In a small bowl, combine the bacon and the bourbon. Refrigerate overnight after sealing. Remove the bacon and pat it dry; toss out the bourbon.
2. Cook bacon in batches in a large frying pan over medium heat until nearly crisp but still flexible. Remove the bacon to a plate lined with paper towels to drain.
3. Separate the dough into 8 rolls and set aside the frosting packet. Spiral rolls should be unrolled into long strips.
4. Place 1 bacon strip on each dough strip, cut as necessary, and reroll to form a spiral. To seal the ends, pinch them together.
5. Press your chosen zone - "Zone 1" or "Zone 2" and then rotate the knob to select "Air Fry".
6. Set the temperature to 175 degrees C, and then set the time for 5 minutes to preheat.
7. After preheating, spray the Air-Fryer basket of each zone with cooking spray, line them with parchment paper, and place rolls.
8. Slide the basket into the Air Fryer and set the time for 5 minutes.
9. Turn the rolls over and cook for another 4 minutes, or until golden brown.
10. Meanwhile, combine the pecans and maple syrup in a mixing bowl. In a separate bowl, combine the contents of the icing packet.
11. Heat the remaining bacon drippings in the same frying pan over medium heat. Cook, stirring regularly until the pecan mixture is gently browned, about 2-3 minutes.
12. After cooking time is completed, transfer them onto serving plates, drizzle of half the icing over warm cinnamon rolls and sprinkle with half the pecans.

Serving Suggestions: Serve them with fruits.
Variation Tip: You can also add a pinch of salt.
Nutritional Information per Serving:
Calories: 267 | Fat: 14g | Sat Fat: 3g | Carbohydrates: 28g | Fibre: 1g | Sugar: 13g | Protein: 5g

Vanilla Cinnamon Rolls

Preparation Time: 25 minutes | Cooking Time: 12 minutes | Servings: 6

Ingredients:

- 420ml warm water
- 300g sugar divided
- 60ml oil
- 2 tablespoons yeast
- ½ tablespoon salt
- 2 eggs
- 625g flour
- 115g butter, softened
- 1 tablespoons cinnamon

For the Frosting:
- 115g butter, softened
- 2 teaspoons vanilla
- 480g icing sugar
- Milk, for desired consistency

Preparation:

1. In the bowl, combine the water, 100g sugar, oil, and yeast; set aside for 15 minutes to allow the yeast to bloom.
2. Combine the salt, eggs, and flour in a mixing bowl. Using the dough hook, mix for 10 minutes. The dough will be slightly damp. Allow 10 minutes for rest.
3. Roll out the dough into a ½ cm thick rectangle on a floured work surface. Spread softened butter around the dough's edges.
4. In a bowl, combine the remaining sugar and the cinnamon.
5. Roll into a tube and cut into 12 pieces lengthwise.
6. Combine the softened butter, vanilla, and icing sugar in a mixing bowl to make the frosting.
7. Press your chosen zone - "Zone 1" or "Zone 2" and then rotate the knob to select "Air Fryer".
8. Set the temperature to 180 degrees C, and then set the time for 5 minutes to preheat.
9. After preheating, arrange cinnamon rolls into the basket of each zone.
10. Slide the baskets into Air Fryer and set the time for 6 minutes.
11. After cooking time is completed, transfer the rolls onto serving plates, top with frosting and serve hot.

Serving Suggestions: Top with your favourite frosting.
Variation Tip: You can skip the frosting.
Nutritional Information per Serving:
Calories: 700 | Fat: 21g | Sat Fat: 10g | Carbohydrates: 122g | Fibre: 2g | Sugar: 81g | Protein: 7g

Banana Bread with Walnuts

Preparation Time: 10 minutes | Cooking Time: 35 minutes | Servings: 8

Ingredients:

- 95g flour
- 1 teaspoon ground cinnamon
- ¼ teaspoon ground nutmeg
- ½ teaspoon salt
- ¼ teaspoon baking soda
- 2 medium-sized ripe bananas mashed
- 2 large eggs lightly beaten
- 100g granulated sugar
- 2 tablespoons whole milk
- 1 tablespoon plain nonfat yoghurt
- 2 tablespoons vegetable oil
- 1 teaspoon vanilla
- 2 tablespoons walnuts roughly chopped

Preparation:

1. Combine flour, cinnamon, nutmeg, baking soda, and salt in a large mixing basin.
2. Mash the banana in a separate dish before adding the eggs, sugar, milk, yoghurt, oil, and vanilla extract.
3. Combine the wet and dry ingredients in a mixing bowl and stir until just incorporated.
4. Pour the batter into the loaf pan, top with chopped walnuts.
5. Press either "Zone 1" and "Zone 2" and then rotate the knob select "Air Fryer".
6. Set the temperature to 155 degrees C, and then set the time for 3 minutes to preheat.
7. After preheating, arrange 1 loaf pan into the basket.
8. Slide basket into Air Fryer and set the time for 35 minutes.
9. After cooking time is completed, remove pan from Air Fryer.
10. Place the loaf pan onto a wire rack, cool for about 10 minutes.
11. Carefully invert the bread onto a wire rack to cool completely before slicing
12. Cut the bread into desired-sized slices and serve.

Serving Suggestions: Top with maple syrup.
Variation Tip: You can serve with fruits.
Nutritional Information per Serving:
Calories: 186 | Fat: 7g | Sat Fat: 3g | Carbohydrates: 29g | Fibre: 1g | Sugar: 17g | Protein: 4g

Raspberry Puff Pastry

Preparation Time: 20 minutes | Cooking Time: 10 minutes | Servings: 6

Ingredients:

- 1 package (200g) cream cheese, softened
- 50g sugar
- 2 tablespoons plain flour
- ½ teaspoon vanilla extract
- 2 large egg yolks
- 1 tablespoon water
- 1 package frozen puff pastry, thawed
- 210g seedless raspberry jam

Preparation:

1. Mix the cream cheese, sugar, flour, and vanilla extract until smooth, then add 1 egg yolk.
2. Combine the remaining egg yolk with the water. Unfold each sheet of puff pastry on a lightly floured board and roll into a 30 cm square. Cut into nine 10 cm squares.
3. Put 1 tablespoon of cream cheese mixture and 1 rounded teaspoon jam on each. Bring 2 opposite corners of pastry over the filling, sealing with yolk mixture.
4. Brush the remaining yolk mixture over the tops.
5. Press your chosen zone - "Zone 1" or "Zone 2" and then rotate the knob to select "Air Fry".
6. Set the temperature to 160 degrees C, and then set the time for 5 minutes to preheat.
7. After preheating, spray the Air-Fryer basket of each zone with cooking spray, line them with parchment paper, and place the pastry on them.
8. Slide the basket into the Air Fryer and set the time for 10 minutes.
9. After cooking time is completed, transfer them onto serving plates and serve.

Serving Suggestions: Serve them with fruits.
Variation Tip: You can use the jam of your choice.
Nutritional Information per Serving:
Calories: 197 | Fat: 12g | Sat Fat: 4g | Carbohydrates: 20g | Fibre: 2g | Sugar: 3g | Protein: 3g

Cinnamon French Toast Sticks

Preparation Time: 5 minutes | Cooking Time: 12 minutes | Servings: 5

Ingredients:

- 10 teaspoons sugar, divided
- 3¼ teaspoons cinnamon, divided
- 3 slices toast
- 1 egg
- 1 egg yolks
- 80ml milk
- 1 teaspoon sugar
- 1 teaspoon brown sugar
- 1 teaspoon vanilla
- ¼ teaspoon cinnamon

Preparation:

1. Line either basket "Zone 1" and "Zone 2" with a greased piece of foil.
2. Press your chosen zone - "Zone 1" and "Zone 2" and then rotate the knob to select "Air Fryer".
3. Set the temperature to 175 degrees C, and then set the time for 3 minutes to preheat.
4. Three teaspoons of sugar and 3 teaspoons of cinnamon are whisked together in a shallow bowl. Set aside.
5. Cut each slice of bread in thirds.
6. Combine the eggs, egg yolks, milk, brown sugar, remaining sugar, vanilla, and remaining cinnamon in a shallow pan.
7. Blend everything until it's smooth.
8. Allow the bread to soak in the egg mixture for a few seconds. Flip over and dip the other side.
9. Coat both sides of the bread in the cinnamon-sugar mixture. Place in the basket.
10. Slide the basket into the Air Fryer and set the time for 8 minutes.
11. After cooking time is completed, transfer the bread to a serving plate and serve.

Serving Suggestions: Top with maple syrup.
Variation Tip: You can serve with fruits.
Nutritional Information per Serving:
Calories: 162 | Fat: 7g | Sat Fat: 2g | Carbohydrates: 22g | Fibre: 2g | Sugar: 12g | Protein: 4g

Egg in a Hole

Preparation Time: 5 minutes | Cooking Time: 8 minutes | Servings: 1

Ingredients:

- 1 tablespoon butter, softened
- 2 eggs
- 2 slices of bread
- Salt and black pepper, to taste

Preparation:

1. Line either basket of "Zone 1" and "Zone 2" with a greased piece of foil.
2. Press your chosen zone - "Zone 1" or "Zone 2" and then rotate the knob to select "Air Fryer".
3. Set the temperature to 160 degrees C, and then set the time for 3 minutes to preheat.
4. After preheating, place the butter on both sides of the bread. Cut a hole in the centre of the bread and crack the egg.
5. Slide the basket into the Air Fryer and set the time for 6 minutes.
6. After cooking time is completed, transfer the bread to a serving plate and serve.

Serving Suggestions: Top with salt and pepper.
Variation Tip: You can serve with veggies.
Nutritional Information per Serving:
Calories: 377 | Fat: 22g | Sat Fat: 10g | Carbohydrates: 28g | Fibre: 2g | Sugar: 4g | Protein: 17g

Avocado Egg Cups

Preparation Time: 15 minutes | Cooking Time: 12 minutes | Servings: 4

Ingredients:

2 avocados, halved and pitted
4 eggs
Salt and ground black pepper, as required

Preparation:

1. Line either basket of "Zone 1" and "Zone 2" of Ninja Foodi 2-Basket Air Fryer with a greased square piece of foil.
2. Press your chosen zone - "Zone 1" and "Zone 2" and then rotate the knob to select "Bake".
3. Set the temperature to 200 degrees C and then set the time for 5 minutes to preheat.
4. Meanwhile, carefully scoop out about 2 teaspoons of flesh from each avocado half.
5. Crack 1 egg in each avocado half and sprinkle with salt and black pepper.
6. After preheating, arrange 2 avocado halves into the basket.
7. Slide the basket into the Air Fryer and set the time for 12 minutes.
8. After cooking time is completed, transfer the avocado halves and onto serving plates and serve hot.

Serving Suggestions: Serve with buttered toasts.
Variation Tip: Don't use over-ripe avocados.
Nutritional Information per Serving:
Calories: 268 | Fat: 24g | Sat Fat: 5.5g | Carbohydrates: 9g | Fibre: 6.7g | Sugar: 0.8g | Protein: 7.5g

Air Fryer Apples with Cinnamon Oats

Preparation Time: 10 minutes | Cooking Time: 15 minutes | Servings: 4

Ingredients:

2 apples, cut in half and cored
2 tablespoons butter, melted
40g oats
3 teaspoons honey
½ teaspoon ground cinnamon

Preparation:

1. Apply the butter to the apple halves' tops.
2. Combine the remaining butter, oats, honey, and cinnamon in a mixing bowl.
3. Distribute the mixture evenly over the apples' tops.
4. Press either "Zone 1" or "Zone 2" and then rotate the knob to select "Air Fryer".
5. Set the temperature to 190 degrees C, and then set the time for 3 minutes to preheat.
6. After preheating, Arrange the apples in the basket.
7. Slide basket into Air Fryer and set the time for 15 minutes.
8. After cooking time is completed, remove basket from Air Fryer.
9. Place them on serving plates and serve.

Serving Suggestions: Top with extra cinnamon sugar.
Variation Tip: You can also top with whipped cream.
Nutritional Information per Serving:
Calories: 153 | Fat: 6g | Sat Fat: 1g | Carbohydrates: 24g | Fibre: 3g | Sugar: 14g | Protein: 2g

Cream Bacon & Spinach Cups

Preparation Time: 15 minutes | Cooking Time: 19 minutes | Servings: 6

Ingredients:

- 6 eggs
- 12 bacon slices, chopped
- 120g fresh baby spinach
- 180g heavy cream
- 6 tablespoons Parmesan cheese, grated
- Salt and ground black pepper, as required

Preparation:

1. Heat a non-stick frying pan over medium-high heat, Cook the bacon for about 6-8 minutes.
2. Add the spinach and cook for about 2-3 minutes.
3. Stir in the Parmesan cheese and heavy cream, cook for about 2-3 minutes.
4. Remove from the heat and set aside to cool slightly.
5. Press "Zone 1" and "Zone 2" of Ninja Foodi 2-Basket Air Fryer and then rotate the knob for each zone to select "Air Fry".
6. Set the temperature to 175 degrees C and then set the time for 5 minutes to preheat.
7. Crack 1 egg in each of 6 greased ramekins and top with bacon mixture.
8. After preheating, arrange 3 ramekins into the basket of each zone.
9. Slide the basket into the Air Fryer and set the time for 5 minutes.
10. After cooking time is completed, remove the ramekins from Air Fryer.
11. Sprinkle the top of each cup with salt and black pepper and serve hot.

Serving Suggestions: Serve with the topping of sour cream.
Variation Tip: You can use greens of your choice.
Nutritional Information per Serving:
Calories: 442 | Fat: 34.5g | Sat Fat: 12.9g | Carbohydrates: 2.3g | Fibre: 0.5g | Sugar: 0.4g | Protein: 26.9g

Spicy Breakfast Potatoes

Preparation Time: 5 minutes | Cooking Time: 20 minutes | Servings: 6

Ingredients:

- 3 russet potatoes, cut into bite-sized pieces with skin on
- 1 teaspoon garlic powder
- 1 teaspoon onion powder
- 2 teaspoons fine ground sea salt
- 1 teaspoon black pepper
- 1 tablespoon olive oil
- ½ red pepper, diced

Preparation:

1. The potatoes should be washed and scrubbed before being sliced into bite-sized pieces with the skin on.
2. Using paper towels, dry them and place them in a large mixing bowl.
3. Toss in the spices and drizzle with olive oil. Stir in the pepper until everything is completely combined.
4. Line a basket with parchment paper.
5. Press either "Zone 1" or "Zone 2" and then rotate the knob to select "Air Fryer".
6. Set the temperature to 195 degrees C, and then set the time for 3 minutes to preheat.
7. After preheating, spread the potatoes in a single layer on the sheet.
8. Slide basket into Air Fryer and set the time for 15 minutes.
9. After cooking time is completed, remove basket from Air Fryer.
10. Place them on serving plates and serve.

Serving Suggestions: Top with parsley.
Variation Tip: You can use any oil.
Nutritional Information per Serving:
Calories: 111 | Fat: 2g | Sat Fat: 1g | Carbohydrates: 21g | Fibre: 2g | Sugar: 1g | Protein: 3g

Salmon Onion Quiche

Preparation Time: 15 minutes | Cooking Time: 20 minutes | Servings: 4

Ingredients:

- 275g salmon fillets, chopped
- Salt and ground black pepper, as required
- 1 tablespoon fresh lemon juice
- 2 egg yolks
- 7 tablespoons chilled butter
- 165g flour
- 2 tablespoons cold water
- 4 eggs
- 6 tablespoons whipping cream
- 2 spring onions, chopped

Preparation:

1. In a bowl, mix together the salmon, salt, black pepper and lemon juice. Set aside.
2. In another bowl, add egg yolk, butter, flour and water and mix until a dough forms.
3. Divide the dough into 2 portions.
4. Place each dough onto a floured smooth surface and roll into about 17.5cm round.
5. Place each rolled dough into a quiche pan and press firmly in the bottom and along the edges.
6. Then trim the excess edges.
7. In a small bowl, add the eggs, cream, salt and black pepper and beat until well combined.
8. Place the cream mixture over each crust evenly and top with the salmon, followed by the spring onion.
9. Press either "Zone 1" or "Zone 2" of Ninja Foodi 2-Basket Air Fryer and then rotate the knob for each zone to select "Air Fry".
10. Set the temperature to 180 degrees C and then set the time for 5 minutes to preheat.
11. After preheating, arrange 1 quiche pan into the basket of each zone.
12. Slide the basket into the Air Fryer and set the time for 20 minutes.
13. After cooking time is completed, remove the quiche pans from Air Fryer.
14. Cut each quiche in 2 portions and serve hot.

Serving Suggestions: Serve with fresh greens.
Variation Tip: Use skinless salmon fillets.
Nutritional Information per Serving:
Calories: 592 | Fat: 39g | Sat Fat: 20.1g | Carbohydrates: 33.8g | Fibre: 1.4g | Sugar: 0.8g | Protein: 27.2g

Sesame Yoghurt Bagels

Preparation Time: 15 minutes | Cooking Time: 12 minutes | Servings: 4

Ingredients:

- 125g plain flour
- 2 teaspoons baking powder
- Salt, as required
- 240g plain Greek yogurt
- 1 egg, beaten
- 1 tablespoon water
- 1 tablespoon sesame seeds
- 1 teaspoon coarse salt

Preparation:

1. In a large bowl, mix together the flour, salt and baking powder.
2. Add the yogurt and mix until a dough ball forms.
3. Place the dough onto a lightly floured surface and then cut into 4 equal-sized balls.
4. Roll each ball into a 17 – 19 cm rope and then join ends to shape a bagel.
5. Grease basket of Ninja Foodi 2-Basket Air Fryer.
6. Press your chosen zone - "Zone 1" or "Zone 2" and then rotate the knob to select "Air Fry".
7. Set the temperature to 165 degrees C and then set the time for 5 minutes to preheat.
8. Meanwhile, add egg and water in a small bowl and mix well.
9. Brush the bagels with egg mixture evenly.
10. Sprinkle the top of each bagel with sesame seeds and salt, pressing lightly.
11. After preheating, arrange 2 bagels into the basket of each zone.
12. Slide the basket into the Air Fryer and set the time for 12 minutes.
13. After cooking time is completed, remove the bagels from Air Fryer and serve warm.

Serving Suggestions: Serve with cream cheese.
Variation Tip: Use room temperature eggs.
Nutritional Information per Serving:
Calories: 188 | Fat: 3.3g | Sat Fat: 1.2g | Carbohydrates: 29.9g | Fibre: 1.2g | Sugar: 4.5g | Protein: 8.5g

Sausage & Bacon Omelet with Onion

Preparation Time: 15 minutes | Cooking Time: 10 minutes | Servings: 4

Ingredients:

- 8 eggs
- 2 bacon slices, chopped
- 4 sausages, chopped
- 2 yellow onions, chopped

Preparation:

1. In a bowl, crack the eggs and beat well.
2. Add the remaining ingredients and gently stir to combine.
3. Divide the mixture into 2 small baking pans.
4. Press your chosen zone - "Zone 1" or "Zone 2" and then rotate the knob to select "Air Fry".
5. Set the temperature to 160 degrees C and then set the time for 5 minutes to preheat.
6. After preheating, arrange 1 pan into the basket of each zone.
7. Slide the basket into the Air Fryer and set the time for 10 minutes.
8. After cooking time is completed, remove the both pans from Air Fryer.
9. Cut each omelet in wedges and serve hot.

Serving Suggestions: Serve with buttered toasts.
Variation Tip: use sausage of your choice.
Nutritional Information per Serving:
Calories: 508 | Fat: 15.6g | Sat Fat: 4.8g | Carbohydrates: 6g | Fibre: 1.2g | Sugar: 3g | Protein: 33.2g

Savory Peppers Soufflé

Preparation Time: 15 minutes | Cooking Time: 8 minutes | Servings: 4

Ingredients:

- 4 tablespoons light cream
- 4 eggs
- 2 tablespoons fresh parsley, chopped
- 2 fresh red chilies pepper, chopped
- Salt, as required

Preparation:

1. In a bowl, add all the ingredients and beat until well combined.
2. Divide the mixture into 4 greased soufflé dishes.
3. Press either "Zone 1" and "Zone 2" of Ninja Foodi 2-Basket Air Fryer and then rotate the knob to select "Air Fry".
4. Set the temperature to 200 degrees C, and then set the time for 5 minutes to preheat.
5. After preheating, arrange soufflé dishes into the basket.
6. Slide basket into Air Fryer and set the time for 8 minutes.
7. After cooking time is completed, remove the soufflé dishes from Air Fryer and serve warm.

Serving Suggestions: Serve with bread slices.
Variation Tip: Feel free to use seasoning of your choice.
Nutritional Information per Serving:
Calories: 108 | Fat: 9g | Sat Fat: 4.3g | Carbohydrates: 1.1g | Fibre: 0.2g | Sugar: 0.5g | Protein: 6g

Baked Parmesan Eggs

Preparation Time: 15 minutes | Cooking Time: 12 minutes | Servings: 10

Ingredients:

450g marinara sauce, divided
2 tablespoons capers, drained and divided
16 eggs
120g whipping cream, divided
50g Parmesan cheese, shredded and divided
Salt and ground black pepper, as required

Preparation:

1. Press "Zone 1" and "Zone 2" and then rotate the knob to select "Bake".
2. Set the temperature to 200 degrees C and then set the time for 5 minutes to preheat.
3. Divide the marinara sauce in the bottom of 8 greased ramekins evenly and top with capers.
4. Carefully crack 2 eggs over marinara sauce into each ramekin and top with cream, followed by the Parmesan cheese.
5. Sprinkle each ramekin with salt and black pepper.
6. After preheating, arrange the ramekins into the basket of each zone.
7. Slide the basket into the Air Fryer and set the time for 12 minutes.
8. After cooking time is completed, remove the ramekins from Air Fryer.
9. Serve hot.

Serving Suggestions: Serve
Nutritional Information per Serving:
Calories: 179 | Fat: 11.3g | Sat Fat: 4.4g | Carbohydrates: 7.8g | Fibre: 1.4g | Sugar: 5.5g | Protein: 11.4g

Homemade French Toasts

Preparation Time: 15 minutes | Cooking Time: 6 minutes | Servings: 4

Ingredients:

4 eggs
120g evaporated milk
6 tablespoons sugar
4 teaspoons olive oil
¼ teaspoon ground cinnamon
¼ teaspoon vanilla extract
8 bread slices

Preparation:

1. Line each basket of "Zone 1" and "Zone 2" with a greased piece of foil.
2. Then Press your chosen zone - "Zone 1" or "Zone 2" and then rotate the knob to select "Air Fry".
3. Set the temperature to 200 degrees C and then set the time for 5 minutes to preheat.
4. In a large bowl, add all ingredients except for bread slices and beat until well combined.
5. Coat the bread slices with egg mixture evenly.
6. After preheating, arrange 4 bread slices into the basket of each zone.
7. Slide the basket into the Air Fryer and set the time for 6 minutes.
8. While cooking, flip the slices once halfway through.
9. After cooking time is completed, remove the French toasts from Air Fryer and serve warm.

Serving Suggestions: Serve with the topping of butter and maple syrup.
Variation Tip: Use thick bread slices.
Calories: 262 | Fat: 12g | Sat Fat: 3.6g | Carbohydrates: 30.8g | Fibre: 0.5g | Sugar: 22.3g | Protein: 9.1g

Banana Blueberry Muffins

Preparation Time: 15 minutes | Cooking Time: 12 minutes | Servings: 12

Ingredients:

- 2 egg, beaten
- 2 ripe bananas, peeled and mashed
- 220g almond flour
- 4 tablespoons granulated sugar
- 1 teaspoon baking powder
- 2 tablespoons coconut oil, melted
- 80g maple syrup
- 2 teaspoons apple cider vinegar
- 2 teaspoons vanilla extract
- 2 teaspoons lemon zest, grated
- Pinch of ground cinnamon
- 150g fresh blueberries

Preparation:

1. In a large bowl, add all the ingredients except blueberries and mix until well combined.
2. Gently fold in the blueberries.
3. Grease 2 (6-cups) muffin tins.
4. Place the mixture into prepared muffin cups about ¾ full.
5. Press your chosen zone - "Zone 1" or "Zone 2" and then rotate the knob to select "Bake".
6. Set the temperature to 190 degrees C and then set the time for 5 minutes to preheat.
7. After preheating, arrange 1 muffin tin into the basket of each zone.
8. Slide the basket into the Air Fryer and set the time for 12 minutes.
9. After cooking time is completed, remove the muffin tins from Air Fryer.
10. Place both tins onto a wire rack to cool for 10 minutes.
11. Invert the blueberry muffins onto the wire rack. Cool completely before serving.

Serving Suggestions: Serve with a cup of coffee.
Variation Tip: For best result use fresh blueberries.
Nutritional Information per Serving:
Calories: 223 | Fat: 14.8g | Sat Fat: 3g | Carbohydrates: 20.1g | Fibre: 3.4g | Sugar: 12.5g | Protein: 6.2g

Simple Hard Boiled Eggs

Preparation Time: 5 minutes | Cooking Time: 18 minutes | Servings: 6

Ingredients:

- 6 eggs
- Cold water

Preparation:

1. Press your chosen zone - "Zone 1" or "Zone 2" and then rotate the knob to select "Air Fryer".
2. Set the temperature to 120 degrees C, and then set the time for 5 minutes to preheat.
3. After preheating, arrange eggs into the basket of each zone.
4. Slide the baskets into Air Fryer and set the time for 18 minutes.
5. After cooking time is completed, transfer the eggs into cold water and serve.

Serving Suggestions: Top with salt and pepper.
Variation Tip: You can serve with avocado.
Nutritional Information per Serving:
Calories: 78 | Fat: 5g | Sat Fat: 1g | Carbohydrates: 1g | Fibre: 0g | Sugar: 1g | Protein: 6g

Chapter 2 Snack and Starter Recipes

Cheese Mushroom Rolls

Preparation Time: 30 minutes | Cooking Time: 10 minutes | Servings: 10

Ingredients:

2 tablespoons olive oil
200g large portobello mushrooms, finely chopped
1 teaspoon dried oregano
½ teaspoon crushed red pepper flakes
¼ teaspoon salt
200g cream cheese, softened
100g whole-milk ricotta cheese
10 flour tortillas
Cooking spray

Preparation:

1. Heat the oil in a frying pan over medium heat. Add the mushrooms and cook for 4 minutes.
2. Sauté until mushrooms are browned, about 4-6 minutes, with oregano, pepper flakes, and salt. Cool.
3. Combine the cheeses in a mixing bowl; fold the mushrooms until thoroughly combined. On the bottom centre of each tortilla, spread 3 tablespoons of the mushroom mixture. Tightly roll up and secure with toothpicks.
4. Press either "Zone 1" or "Zone 2" and then rotate the knob to select "Air Fry".
5. Set the temperature to 200 degrees C, and then set the time for 5 minutes to preheat.
6. After preheating, spray the basket with cooking spray and arrange rolls onto basket.
7. Slide the basket into the Air Fryer and set the time for 10 minutes.
8. After cooking time is completed, transfer them onto serving plates and serve.

Serving Suggestions: Serve with any sauce.
Variation Tip: You can also add dried thyme.
Nutritional Information per Serving:
Calories: 291 | Fat: 16g | Sat Fat: 7g | Carbohydrates: 31g | Fibre: 2g | Sugar: 2g | Protein: 8g

Spicy Beef Skewers

Preparation Time: 20 minutes | Cooking Time: 5 minutes | Servings: 6

Ingredients:

1 beef flank steak
240ml rice vinegar
240ml soy sauce
55g packed brown sugar
2 tablespoons minced fresh
gingerroot
6 garlic cloves, minced
3 teaspoons sesame oil
1 teaspoon hot pepper sauce
½ teaspoon cornflour

Preparation:

1. Cut beef into ½ cm thick strips. Whisk together the following 7 ingredients in a large mixing bowl until well combined.
2. In a shallow dish, pour 1 cup of marinade. Toss in the beef and turn to coat. Refrigerate for 2-8 hours, covered. Cover and keep the remaining marinade refrigerated.
3. Beef should be drained. 12 metal or wet wooden skewers threaded with beef.
4. Press either "Zone 1" or "Zone 2" and then rotate the knob to select "Air Fry".
5. Set the temperature to 200 degrees C, and then set the time for 5 minutes to preheat.
6. After preheating, spray the basket with cooking spray and arrange skewers onto basket.
7. Slide the basket into the Air Fryer and set the time for 5 minutes.
8. After cooking time is completed, transfer them onto serving plates and serve.

Serving Suggestions: Sprinkle sesame seeds on top.
Variation Tip: You can also top with thinly sliced green onions.
Nutritional Information per Serving:
Calories: 254 | Fat: 10g | Sat Fat: 4g | Carbohydrates: 18g | Fibre: 0g | Sugar: 15g | Protein: 24g

Spicy Pumpkin Fries

Preparation Time: 25 minutes | Cooking Time: 15 minutes | Servings: 4

Ingredients:

120g plain Greek yoghurt
2 to 3 teaspoons minced chipotle peppers
⅛ teaspoon plus ½ teaspoon salt, divided
1 medium pie pumpkin
¼ teaspoon garlic powder
¼ teaspoon ground cumin
¼ teaspoon chili powder
¼ teaspoon pepper

Preparation:

1. Combine yoghurt, chipotle peppers, and ⅛ teaspoon salt in a small bowl. Refrigerate until ready to serve, covered.
2. Peeled the pumpkin and split it in half lengthwise. Discard the seeds. Cut pumpkin into 1 cm strips.
3. Place in a large mixing bowl. Toss with ½ teaspoon salt, garlic powder, cumin, chili powder, and pepper.
4. Press either "Zone 1" or "Zone 2" and then rotate the knob to select "Air Fry".
5. Set the temperature to 200 degrees C, and then set the time for 5 minutes to preheat.
6. After preheating, spray the Air-Fryer basket with cooking spray and line with parchment paper. Arrange pumpkin fries and spritz cooking spray on them.
7. Slide the basket into the Air Fryer and set the time for 8 minutes.
8. After that, toss them and again cook for 3 minutes longer.
9. After cooking time is completed, transfer them onto serving plates and serve.

Serving Suggestions: Serve with chili sauce.
Variation Tip: You can also add 2 tbsp. maple syrup.
Nutritional Information per Serving:
Calories: 151 | Fat: 3g | Sat Fat: 2g | Carbohydrates: 31g | Fibre: 2g | Sugar: 12g | Protein: 5g

Garlic Butter Bread

Preparation Time: 10 minutes | Cooking Time: 10 minutes | Servings: 8

Ingredients:

60g butter, softened
3 tablespoons grated Parmesan cheese
2 garlic cloves, minced
2 teaspoons minced fresh parsley
8 slices of French bread

Preparation:

1. Press either "Zone 1" or "Zone 2" and then rotate the knob to select "Bake".
2. Set the temperature to 175 degrees C, and then set the time for 5 minutes to preheat.
3. After preheating, combine the first four ingredients in a small mixing bowl; spread on bread. Arrange bread slices onto basket.
4. Slide the basket into the Air Fryer and set the time for 3 minutes.
5. After cooking time is completed, transfer them onto serving plates and serve.

Serving Suggestions: Serve with avocado on top.
Variation Tip: You can also use dried parsley flakes instead of fresh ones.
Nutritional Information per Serving:
Calories: 122 | Fat: 7g | Sat Fat: 4g | Carbohydrates: 14g | Fibre: 1g | Sugar: 1g | Protein: 3g

Beef Mushroom Pastry

Preparation Time: 20 minutes | Cooking Time: 10 minutes | Servings: 4

Ingredients:

455g of beef mince	¼ teaspoon pepper
70g sliced fresh mushrooms	1 sheet frozen puff pastry, thawed
80g chopped onion	
1-½ teaspoons minced garlic	151g refrigerated mashed potatoes
¾ teaspoon dried rosemary, crushed	100g shredded Swiss cheese
¾ teaspoon paprika	1 large egg
½ teaspoon salt	2 tablespoons water

Preparation:

1. Cook the beef, mushrooms, and onion in a large frying pan over medium heat until the meat is no longer pink and the veggies are cooked, 8-10 minutes; crumble the meat.
2. Cook for a further minute after adding the garlic. Drain. Season with salt and pepper. Remove the pan from the heat, set aside.
3. Place the puff pastry on a lightly floured surface and roll into a rectangle. Make four little rectangles out of the dough.
4. Over each square, spread around 2 teaspoons of potatoes. ¾ cup beef mixture on top of each; 25g cheese on each.
5. In a small bowl, whisk the egg and water; brush the wash over the pastry edges.
6. Bring opposing pastry corners over each bundle and pinch seams together to seal. Brush with the rest of the egg mixture.
7. Press either "Zone 1" or "Zone 2" and then rotate the knob to select "Air Fry".
8. Set the temperature to 190 degrees C, and then set the time for 5 minutes to preheat.
9. After preheating, spray the Air-Fryer basket with cooking spray and line with parchment paper. Arrange pastry in a single layer and spray them with cooking spray.
10. Slide the basket into the Air Fryer and set the time for 10 minutes.
11. After that, turn them and again cook for 3 minutes longer.
12. After cooking time is completed, transfer them onto serving plates and serve.

Serving Suggestions: Serve with your favourite sauce.
Variation Tip: You can add spices of your choice.
Nutritional Information per Serving:
Calories: 706 | Fat: 42g | Sat Fat: 15g | Carbohydrates: 44g | Fibre: 2g | Sugar: 6g | Protein: 35g

Cheese Turkey Croquettes

Preparation Time: 20 minutes | Cooking Time: 10 minutes | Servings: 6

Ingredients:

460g mashed potatoes	¼ teaspoon pepper
50g grated Parmesan cheese	420g finely chopped cooked turkey
50g shredded Swiss cheese	
1 shallot, finely chopped	1 large egg
2 teaspoons minced fresh rosemary	2 tablespoons water
	110g panko bread crumbs
½ teaspoon salt	Cooking spray

Preparation:

1. Combine mashed potatoes, rosemary, cheeses, shallot, salt, and pepper in a large mixing bowl; stir in turkey.
2. Lightly but completely combine the ingredients. Form into twelve 2.5cm thick patties.
3. Whisk the egg and water together in a small basin. In a shallow bowl, place the bread crumbs.
4. Dip the croquettes in the egg mixture, then in the bread crumbs, patting them down.
5. Press either "Zone 1" or "Zone 2" and then rotate the knob to select "Air Fry".
6. Set the temperature to 190 degrees C, and then set the time for 5 minutes to preheat.
7. After preheating, spray the Air-Fryer basket with cooking spray and line with parchment paper. Arrange in a single layer and spritz them with cooking spray.
8. Slide the basket into the Air Fryer and set the time for 5 minutes.
9. After that, turn them and again cook for 5 minutes longer.
10. After cooking time is completed, transfer them onto serving plates and serve.

Serving Suggestions: Serve with your favourite sauce.
Variation Tip: You can use any cheese.
Nutritional Information per Serving:
Calories: 322 | Fat: 12g | Sat Fat: 6g | Carbohydrates: 22g | Fibre: 2g | Sugar: 2g | Protein: 29g

Crispy Breaded Calamari Rings

Preparation Time: 5 minutes | Cooking Time: 10 minutes | Servings: 4

Ingredients:

- 455g calamari rings, patted dry
- 3 tablespoons lemon juice
- 60g plain flour
- 1 teaspoon garlic powder
- 2 egg whites
- 60ml milk
- 220g panko breadcrumbs
- 1½ teaspoon salt
- 1½ teaspoon ground black pepper

Preparation:

1. Allow the squid rings to marinade for at least 30 minutes in a bowl with lemon juice. Drain the water in a colander.
2. In a shallow bowl, combine the flour and garlic powder.
3. In a separate bowl, whisk together the egg whites and milk.
4. In a third bowl, combine the panko breadcrumbs, salt, and pepper.
5. Floured first the calamari rings, then dip in the egg mixture, and finally in the panko breadcrumb mixture.
6. Press either "Zone 1" or "Zone 2" and then rotate the knob to select "Air Fry".
7. Set the temperature to 200 degrees C, and then set the time for 5 minutes to preheat.
8. After preheating, spray the Air-Fryer basket with cooking spray and line with parchment paper. Arrange in a single layer and spritz them with cooking spray.
9. Slide the basket into the Air Fryer and set the time for 10 minutes.
10. After cooking time is completed, transfer them onto serving plates and serve.

Serving Suggestions: Serve with chili sauce.
Variation Tip: You can also serve lemon wedges with them.
Nutritional Information per Serving:
Calories: 591 | Fat: 15g | Sat Fat: 2g | Carbohydrates: 87g | Fibre: 5g | Sugar: 7g | Protein: 26g

Cheese Spinach Patties

Preparation Time: 20 minutes | Cooking Time: 10 minutes | Servings: 4

Ingredients:

- 2 large eggs
- 250g frozen spinach, thawed, squeezed dry and chopped
- 185g crumbled feta cheese
- 2 garlic cloves, minced
- ¼ teaspoon pepper
- 1 tube (345g) refrigerated pizza crust

Preparation:

1. Whisk eggs in a mixing bowl, reserving 1 tbsp. Combine the spinach, feta cheese, garlic, pepper, and the rest of the beaten eggs in a mixing bowl.
2. Roll out the pizza crust into a 30cm square. Cut each square into four 15cm squares.
3. Place about ⅓ cup of spinach mixture on each square. Fold them into a triangle and pinch them together to seal the edges. Make slits on the top and brush with the remaining egg.
4. Press either "Zone 1" and "Zone 2" and then rotate the knob to select "Air Fry".
5. Set the temperature to 220 degrees C, and then set the time for 5 minutes to preheat.
6. After preheating, spray the Air-Fryer basket with cooking spray and line with parchment paper. Arrange in a single layer and spritz them with cooking spray.
7. Slide the basket into the Air Fryer and set the time for 10 minutes.
8. After cooking time is completed, transfer them onto serving plates and serve.

Serving Suggestions: Serve with your tzatziki sauce.
Variation Tip: You can use any cheese.
Nutritional Information per Serving:
Calories: 361 | Fat: 9g | Sat Fat: 9g | Carbohydrates: 51g | Fibre: 4g | Sugar: 7g | Protein: 17g

Breaded Mozzarella Sticks

Preparation Time: 10 minutes | Cooking Time: 6 minutes | Servings: 6

Ingredients:

- 150g block Mozzarella cheese or string cheese
- 6 slices of white bread
- 1 large egg
- 1 tablespoon water
- 55g panko breadcrumbs
- 1 tablespoon olive oil

Preparation:

1. Remove the crust from the bread. Discard or save for breadcrumbs.
2. Roll the bread into thin slices with a rolling pin.
3. Slice mozzarella into 30 cm x 10 cm -long sticks, nearly the same size as your bread slices.
4. In a small bowl, whisk together the egg and the water.
5. Fill a shallow pie plate halfway with panko.
6. Wrap a bread slice around each mozzarella stick.
7. Brush the egg wash around the edge of the bread and push to seal it. Brush all over the bread outside.
8. Dredge in Panko and push to coat on all sides.
9. Line basket with parchment paper.
10. Press either "Zone 1" or "Zone 2" and then rotate the knob to select "Air Fryer".
11. Set the temperature to 200 degrees C, and then set the time for 5 minutes to preheat.
12. After preheating, arrange sticks into the basket.
13. Slide the basket into the Air Fryer and set the time for 6 minutes.
14. After cooking time is completed, place on a wire rack for a few minutes, then transfer onto serving plates and serve.

Serving Suggestions: Serve with marinara sauce.
Variation Tip: You can use any cheese.
Nutritional Information per Serving:
Calories: 282 | Fat: 6g | Sat Fat: 8g | Carbohydrates: 25g | Fibre: 2g | Sugar: 4g | Protein: 13g

Easy Potato Fries

Preparation Time: 5 minutes | Cooking Time: 12 minutes | Servings: 2

Ingredients:

- 3 medium russet potatoes, sliced
- 1 teaspoon olive oil
- Salt and pepper, to taste

Preparation:

1. Potatoes should be washed and dried. Cut them into ½ cm slices.
2. Soak the slices in cold water for 3 minutes to remove the starch.
3. Remove the potatoes from the water and pat them dry. Toss them in a bowl with olive oil, pepper and a pinch of salt.
4. Press either "Zone 1" or "Zone 2" and then rotate the knob to select "Air Fryer".
5. Set the temperature to 200 degrees C, and then set the time for 5 minutes to preheat.
6. After preheating, arrange potatoes into the basket.
7. Slide the basket into the Air Fryer and set the time for 12 minutes.
8. While cooking, toss the potato pieces once halfway through.
9. After cooking time is completed, transfer the fries onto serving plates and serve.

Serving Suggestions: Serve with any sauce.
Variation Tip: You can sprinkle parsley on top.
Nutritional Information per Serving:
Calories: 272 | Fat: 3g | Sat Fat: 1g | Carbohydrates: 12g | Fibre: 4g | Sugar: 2g | Protein: 7g

Homemade Soft Pretzels

Preparation Time: 15 minutes | Cooking Time: 6 minutes | Servings: 8

Ingredients:

360ml warm water
1 tablespoon dry active yeast
1 tablespoon sugar
1 tablespoon olive oil
500g plain flour
1 teaspoon salt
1 large egg
1 tablespoon water

Preparation:

1. Combine warm water, yeast, sugar, and olive oil in a large mixing bowl. Stir everything together and leave aside for about 5 minutes.
2. Add 375g flour and a teaspoon of salt to the mixture. Stir well.
3. Roll out the dough on a floured surface. Knead for 3 to 5 minutes, or until the dough is no longer sticky, adding 1 tablespoon of flour at a time if necessary.
4. The dough should be divided in half. At a time, work with half of the dough.
5. Each dough half should be divided into eight pieces.
6. Make a 45cm rope out of the dough. Make a U shape out of the dough. Twist the ends two more times.
7. Fold the ends of the dough over the spherical portion.
8. In a small mixing dish, whisk the egg and a tablespoon of water.
9. Brush the egg wash on both sides of the pretzel dough.
10. Press your chosen zone - "Zone 1" or "Zone 2" and then rotate the knob to select "Air Fryer".
11. Set the temperature to 185 degrees C, and then set the time for 5 minutes to preheat.
12. After preheating, arrange pretzels into the basket of each zone.
13. Slide the baskets into Air Fryer and set the time for 6 minutes.
14. After cooking time is completed, place on a wire rack for a few minutes, then transfer onto serving plates and serve.

Serving Suggestions: Serve with any sauce.
Variation Tip: Before air frying, you can sprinkle flake salt over the pretzels.
Nutritional Information per Serving:
Calories: 450 | Fat: 3g | Sat Fat: 1g | Carbohydrates: 88g | Fibre: 3g | Sugar: 1g | Protein: 15g

Easy Pretzels Dogs

Preparation Time: 5 minutes | Cooking Time: 15 minutes | Servings: 8

Ingredients:

180ml warm water
2¼ teaspoons instant yeast
1 teaspoon sugar
2 teaspoons olive oil
250g plain flour
½ teaspoon salt
1 large egg
1 tablespoon water
8 hot dogs

Preparation:

1. Combine warm water, yeast, sugar, and olive oil in a large mixing basin to make the dough.
2. Stir everything together and leave aside for about 5 minutes.
3. Mix in roughly 125g flour and a pinch of salt. Add 125g of flour at a time until the dough comes together into a ball and pulls away from the bowl's sides.
4. On a floured board, pour the dough. Knead the dough for 3 to 5 minutes, adding extra flour until it is no longer sticky.
5. Cut the dough into eight pieces.
6. Roll the dough between your hands, and roll each piece into an 20 cm to 25 cm rope.
7. Pat, the hot dogs, dry with paper towels to make wrapping the dough around them easier.
8. Begin wrapping the dough around one end of each hot dog in a spiral. To seal the ends, pinch them together.
9. In a small mixing dish, whisk together an egg and a tablespoon of water. Coat the dough in egg wash from all sides.
10. Press your chosen zone - "Zone 1" or "Zone 2" and then rotate the knob to select "Air Fryer".
11. Set the temperature to 200 degrees C, and then set the time for 5 minutes to preheat.
12. After preheating, arrange pretzels into the basket of each zone.
13. Slide the baskets into Air Fryer and set the time for 8 minutes.
14. After cooking time is completed, place on a wire rack for a few minutes, then transfer onto serving plates and serve.

Serving Suggestions: Serve with any sauce.
Variation Tip: You can sprinkle the tops of the dough with bagel seasoning.
Nutritional Information per Serving:
Calories: 351 | Fat: 16g | Sat Fat: 16 | Carbohydrates: 38g | Fibre: 1g | Sugar: 1g | Protein: 7g

Air Fryer Cheese Chicken Wings

Preparation Time: 10 minutes | Cooking Time: 30 minutes | Servings: 4

Ingredients:

- 900g chicken wings
- 1 tablespoon olive oil
- 1 tablespoon baking powder
- ½ teaspoon salt
- ½ teaspoon garlic powder
- ½ teaspoon onion powder
- ¼ teaspoon paprika
- ¼ teaspoon black pepper
- 5 tablespoons unsalted butter, melted
- 4-5 cloves garlic, minced
- 25g grated parmesan cheese

Preparation:

1. Using paper towels, fully dry the wings and lay them in a large mixing bowl. Toss them in olive oil and toss to coat.
2. Combine the baking powder, onion powder, salt, garlic powder, paprika, and pepper in a small bowl. Toss the wings in the mixture to evenly coat them.
3. Press your chosen zone - "Zone 1" or "Zone 2" and then rotate the knob to select "Air Fry".
4. Set the temperature to 200 degrees C, and then set the time for 5 minutes to preheat.
5. After preheating, spray the Air-Fryer basket of each zone with cooking spray, place chicken wings in a single layer, and spritz them with cooking spray.
6. Slide the basket into the Air Fryer and set the time for 15 minutes.
7. Carefully flip the wings and cook for 5 to 8 more minutes.
8. Meanwhile, in a microwave-safe bowl, melt the butter. Combine the minced garlic and parmesan cheese in a mixing bowl.
9. After cooking time is completed, combine with the garlic butter in a large mixing dish and serve on a serving plate

Serving Suggestions: Garnish with parsley.
Variation Tip: You can also serve lemon wedges with them.
Nutritional Information per Serving:
Calories: 625 | Fat: 15g | Sat Fat: 50g | Carbohydrates: 17g | Fibre: 17g | Sugar: 0g | Protein: 27g

Cheese Beef Taquitos

Preparation Time: 10 minutes | Cooking Time: 6 minutes | Servings: 8

Ingredients:

- 455g lean beef mince
- 1 teaspoon salt
- 70g salsa
- ½ teaspoon granulated garlic
- ½ teaspoon chili powder
- ½ teaspoon cumin
- 100g shredded cheese
- 12 mini corn tortillas

Preparation:

1. Season beef mince with salt in a frying pan and cook over medium-high heat.
2. Cook until the meat is nicely browned, stirring frequently and breaking it into fine crumbles. Remove from the heat and drain any remaining grease.
3. Stir in the salsa, garlic, chili powder, cumin, and cheese until all ingredients are completely incorporated, and the cheese has melted.
4. Warm tortillas on a grill or iron frying pan to make them flexible. Allow them to warm rather than crisp and brown.
5. Fill each tortilla with about 1 to 2 tablespoons of the meat mixture and roll it up.
6. Press either "Zone 1" or "Zone 2" and then rotate the knob to select "Air Fryer".
7. Set the temperature to 175 degrees C, and then set the time for 5 minutes to preheat.
8. After preheating, arrange them into the basket.
9. Slide the basket into the Air Fryer and set the time for 6 minutes.
10. After cooking time is completed, place on a wire rack for a few minutes, then transfer onto serving plates and serve.

Serving Suggestions: Serve with ketchup.
Variation Tip: You can use any cheese.
Nutritional Information per Serving:
Calories: 427 | Fat: 15g | Sat Fat: 6g | Carbohydrates: 49g | Fibre: 7g | Sugar: 1g | Protein: 26g

Crispy Fried Okra

Preparation Time: 5 minutes | Cooking Time: 10 minutes | Servings: 4

Ingredients:

455g fresh okra
240ml buttermilk
125g plain flour
160g polenta
1 teaspoon salt
1 teaspoon fresh ground pepper

Preparation:

1. Wash and trim the ends of the okra before slicing it into 30cm chunks.
2. In a small dish, pour the buttermilk.
3. Combine flour, polenta, salt, and pepper in a separate dish.
4. Coat all sides of okra slices in buttermilk and then in flour mixture.
5. Place a baking sheet on the baskets.
6. Press either "Zone 1" or "Zone 2" and then rotate the knob to select "Air Fryer".
7. Set the temperature to 175 degrees C, and then set the time for 5 minutes to preheat.
8. After preheating, arrange them into the basket.
9. Slide the basket into the Air Fryer and set the time for 8 minutes.
10. After cooking time is completed, place on a wire rack for a few minutes, then transfer onto serving plates and serve.

Serving Suggestions: Season with salt.
Variation Tip: You can also use chili flakes.
Nutritional Information per Serving:
Calories: 275 | Fat: 2g | Sat Fat: 1g | Carbohydrates: 56g | Fibre: 6g | Sugar: 6g | Protein: 10g

Potato Waffle Fries

Preparation Time: 10 minutes | Cooking Time: 15 minutes | Servings: 2

Ingredients:

2 russet potatoes
½ teaspoon seasoning salt

Preparation:

1. If desired, peel the potatoes.
2. With Wave-Waffle Cutter, slice potatoes by turning them one-quarter turn after each pass over the blade.
3. In a mixing dish, toss the potato pieces with the seasoning salt. Toss the potatoes in the seasoning to ensure that it is uniformly distributed.
4. Place a baking sheet on the baskets.
5. Press either "Zone 1" or "Zone 2" and then rotate the knob to select "Air Fryer".
6. Set the temperature to 200 degrees C, and then set the time for 5 minutes to preheat.
7. After preheating, arrange them into the basket.
8. Slide the basket into the Air Fryer and set the time for 15 minutes.
9. After cooking time is completed, place on a wire rack for a few minutes, then transfer onto serving plates and serve.

Serving Suggestions: Serve with any sauce.
Variation Tip: You can also sprinkle parsley on top.
Nutritional Information per Serving:
Calories: 164 | Fat: 0.2g | Sat Fat: 1g | Carbohydrates: 37g | Fibre: 4g | Sugar: 2g | Protein: 5g

Cumin Potato Tacos

Preparation Time: 20 minutes | **Cooking Time:** 15 minutes | **Servings:** 6

Ingredients:

- 5 small russet potatoes
- 24 mini corn tortillas
- 2 tablespoons rapeseed oil
- ½ teaspoon ground cumin
- ½ teaspoon smoked paprika
- ½ teaspoon granulated garlic
- Salt and pepper, to taste
- 24 long toothpicks

Preparation:

1. Fill a pot halfway with cold water and add entire potatoes. Bring to a boil over high heat, then reduce the heat to medium-high and simmer until fork-tender, about 15 minutes.
2. It takes about 15-20 minutes. Drain and allow to cool slightly before peeling.
3. In a bowl, combine peeled potatoes and seasonings. Mash until the mixture is relatively smooth. Season to taste.
4. Heat tortillas in a large frying pan until warm and malleable. Cover with a towel while you finish heating the rest of the tortillas.
5. On half of a tortilla, spread roughly one heaping tablespoon of mash. Fold it in half and weave a toothpick through it to seal it.
6. Brush the tacos lightly with oil on both sides.
7. Press your chosen zone - "Zone 1" or "Zone 2" and then rotate the knob to select "Air Fryer".
8. Set the temperature to 200 degrees C, and then set the time for 5 minutes to preheat.
9. After preheating, arrange them into the basket of each zone.
10. Slide the baskets into Air Fryer and set the time for 15 minutes.
11. After cooking time is completed, place on a wire rack for a few minutes, then transfer onto serving plates and serve.

Serving Suggestions: Serve with mustard sauce.
Variation Tip: You can use any oil.
Nutritional Information per Serving:
Calories: 220 | Fat: 6g | Sat Fat: 1g | Carbohydrates: 42g | Fibre: 1g | Sugar: 2g | Protein: 6g

Crispy Avocado Fries

Preparation Time: 15 minutes | **Cooking Time:** 10 minutes | **Servings:** 8

Ingredients:

- 60g plain flour
- Salt and ground black pepper, as required
- 2 eggs
- 1 teaspoon water
- 100g seasoned breadcrumbs
- 2 avocados, peeled, pitted and sliced into 8 pieces
- Non-stick cooking spray

Preparation:

1. In a shallow bowl, mix together the flour, salt, and black pepper.
2. In a second bowl, add the egg and water and beat well.
3. In a third bowl, place the breadcrumbs.
4. Coat the avocado slices with flour mixture, then dip into egg mixture and finally, coat evenly with the breadcrumbs.
5. Now, spray the avocado slices with cooking spray evenly.
6. Grease one basket of Ninja Foodi 2-Basket Air Fryer.
7. Press either "Zone 1" and "Zone 2" and then rotate the knob to select "Air Fry".
8. Set the temperature to 200 degrees C and then set the time for 5 minutes to preheat.
9. After preheating, arrange the avocado slices into the basket.
10. Slide basket into Air Fryer and set the time for 10 minutes.
11. After cooking time is completed, remove the fries from Air Fryer and serve warm.

Serving Suggestions: Serve with yogurt dip.
Variation Tip: Don't use over-ripe avocados.
Nutritional Information per Serving:
Calories: 202 | Fat: 12.7g | Sat Fat: 2.4g | Carbohydrates: 18.9g | Fibre: 4.1g | Sugar: 0.4g | Protein: 4.6g

Spicy Cauliflower Poppers

Preparation Time: 15 minutes | Cooking Time: 20 minutes | Servings: 6

Ingredients:

- 3 tablespoons olive oil
- 1 teaspoon paprika
- ⅛ teaspoon cayenne pepper
- ½ teaspoon ground cumin
- ¼ teaspoon ground turmeric
- Salt and ground black pepper, as required
- 1 medium head cauliflower, cut into florets

Preparation:

1. Press "Zone 1" and "Zone 2" of Ninja Foodi 2-Basket Air Fryer and then rotate the knob for each zone to select "Bake".
2. Set the temperature to 230 degrees C and then set the time for 5 minutes to preheat.
3. In a bowl, place all ingredients and toss to coat well.
4. Divide the cauliflower mixture into 2 greased baking pans.
5. After preheating, arrange 1 baking pan into the basket of each zone.
6. Slide the basket into the Air Fryer and set the time for 20 minutes.
7. While cooking, flip the cauliflower mixture once halfway through.
8. After cooking time is completed, remove the baking pans from Air Fryer and serve the cauliflower poppers warm.

Serving Suggestions: Serve with the garnishing of parsley.

Variation Tip: Cut the cauliflower into uniform-sized florets.

Nutritional Information per Serving:
Calories: 73 | Fat: 7.2g | Sat Fat: 1g | Carbohydrates: 2.7g | Fibre: 1.3g | Sugar: 1.1g | Protein: 1g

Fresh Kale Chips

Preparation Time: 15 minutes | Cooking Time: 3 minutes | Servings: 4

Ingredients:

- 1 head fresh kale, stems and ribs removed and cut into 4cm pieces
- 1 tablespoon olive oil
- 1 teaspoon soy sauce
- ⅛ teaspoon cayenne pepper
- Pinch of freshly ground black pepper

Preparation:

1. Add all the ingredients in a large bowl and mix well.
2. Grease basket of Ninja Foodi 2-Basket Air Fryer.
3. Press your chosen zone - "Zone 1" or "Zone 2" and then rotate the knob to select "Air Fry".
4. Set the temperature to 200 degrees C and then set the time for 5 minutes to preheat.
5. After preheating, arrange the kale pieces into the basket of each zone.
6. Slide the basket into the Air Fryer and set the time for 3 minutes.
7. While cooking, toss the kale pieces once halfway through.
8. After cooking time is completed, remove the kale chips and baking pans from Air Fryer.
9. Place the kale chips onto a wire rack to cool for about 10 minutes before serving.

Serving Suggestions: Serve with the sprinkling of coarse salt.

Variation Tip: Pat dry the kale leaves before using.

Nutritional Information per Serving:
Calories: 55 | Fat: 3.5g | Sat Fat: 0.5g | Carbohydrates: 5.3g | Fibre: 0.8g | Sugar: 0g | Protein: 1.6g

Chapter 3 Vegetable and Sides Recipes

Cheese & Brown Rice Stuffed Tomatoes

Preparation Time: 10 minutes | Cooking Time: 15 minutes | Servings: 4

Ingredients:

- 4 medium tomatoes
- Olive oil
- 150g cooked brown rice
- 35g freshly grated Parmesan cheese
- 90g crumbled goat cheese
- 35g chopped toasted walnuts
- 2 tablespoons chopped fresh basil, divided
- 2 cloves garlic, minced
- 25g Italian-seasoned bread crumbs, divided
- 1 tablespoon olive oil

Preparation:

1. Cut the tops off tomatoes and scoop out the flesh, leaving ½ - 1 cm thick sides and bottoms
2. Combine cooked rice, Parmesan cheese, goat cheese, walnuts, 1 tablespoon basil, and garlic in a medium mixing bowl.
3. In a small bowl, combine bread crumbs and 1 tablespoon of olive oil. Fill tomatoes halfway with rice mixture, then top with bread crumb topping.
4. Press either "Zone 1" or "Zone 2" and then rotate the knob to select "Air Fry".
5. Set the temperature to 185 degrees C, and then set the time for 5 minutes to preheat.
6. After preheating, spray the Air-Fryer basket with cooking spray, and arrange them.
7. Slide the basket into the Air Fryer and set the time for 15 minutes.
8. After cooking time is completed, place them on a serving plate and serve.

Serving Suggestions: Sprinkle lemon juice on top.
Variation Tip: You can use any cheese.
Nutritional Information per Serving:
Calories: 255 | Fat: 14g | Sat Fat: 4g | Carbohydrates: 23g | Fibre: 3g | Sugar: 4g | Protein: 8g

Spicy Fried Green Tomatoes

Preparation Time: 15 minutes | Cooking Time: 7 minutes | Servings: 4

Ingredients:

- 3-4 green tomatoes
- ½ teaspoon salt
- 65g flour
- 2 eggs
- 50g polenta
- 35g breadcrumbs
- ⅛ teaspoon paprika
- Cayenne pepper

Preparation:

1. Slice the green tomatoes into ½ cm slices and generously coat with salt. Allow for at least 5 minutes of resting time.
2. Put the flour in one bowl, the egg (whisked) in the second, and the polenta, breadcrumbs, paprika, and cayenne pepper in the third bowl to make a breading station.
3. Using a paper towel, pat green tomato slices dry.
4. Dip each tomato slice into the flour, the egg, and finally the polenta mixture, making sure the tomato slices are completely covered.
5. Press either "Zone 1" or "Zone 2" and then rotate the knob to select "Air Fryer".
6. Set the temperature to 195 degrees C, and then set the time for 5 minutes to preheat.
7. After preheating, arrange them into the basket.
8. Slide the basket into the Air Fryer and set the time for 8 minutes.
9. After cooking time is completed, transfer onto serving plates and serve.

Serving Suggestions: Serve with marinara sauce.
Variation Tip: You can also use cayenne pepper.
Nutritional Information per Serving:
Calories: 186 | Fat: 4g | Sat Fat: 1g | Carbohydrates: 31g | Fibre: 4g | Sugar: 4g | Protein: 8g

Avocado Tacos with Veggie

Preparation Time: 30 minutes | Cooking Time: 10 minutes | Servings: 4

Ingredients:

- 40g shredded fresh kale
- 5g minced fresh coriander
- 60g plain Greek yoghurt
- 2 tablespoons lime juice
- ¼ teaspoon salt
- ¼ teaspoon ground chipotle pepper
- ¼ teaspoon pepper

Tacos:
- 1 large egg, beaten
- 40g polenta
- ½ teaspoon salt
- ½ teaspoon garlic powder
- ½ teaspoon ground chipotle pepper
- 2 medium avocados, peeled and sliced
- Cooking spray
- 8 flour tortillas or corn tortillas
- 1 medium tomato, chopped

Preparation:

1. In a mixing bowl, combine the first 7 ingredients. Refrigerate until ready to serve, covered.
2. In a shallow bowl, crack the egg. Combine polenta, salt, garlic powder, and chipotle pepper in a shallow bowl.
3. Dip avocado slices in the egg, then into the polenta mixture, carefully rubbing them down to help them stick.
4. Press your chosen zone - "Zone 1" or "Zone 2" and then rotate the knob to select "Air Fry".
5. Set the temperature to 200 degrees C, and then set the time for 5 minutes to preheat.
6. After preheating, spray the Air-Fryer basket of each zone with cooking spray and avocado slices in a single layer.
7. Slide the basket into the Air Fryer and set the time for 5 minutes.
8. Carefully turn them and cook for 5 more minutes.
9. After cooking time is completed, serve avocado slices in tortillas with kale mix, tomato, and additional minced coriander and place them on a serving plate and serve.

Serving Suggestions: Sprinkle parsley on top.
Variation Tip: You can add more chopped veggies.
Nutritional Information per Serving:
Calories: 407 | Fat: 21g | Sat Fat: 5g | Carbohydrates: 48g | Fibre: 9g | Sugar: 4g | Protein: 9g

Baked Balsamic Brussel Sprouts

Preparation Time: 10 minutes | Cooking Time: 10 minutes | Servings: 2

Ingredients:

- 455g Brussels sprouts, trimmed and halved
- 1 tablespoon extra-virgin olive oil
- ½ teaspoon garlic powder
- 1 tablespoon balsamic vinegar
- ¼ teaspoon salt, to taste
- ⅛ teaspoon black pepper

Preparation:

1. Brussels sprouts should be rinsed and dried with a kitchen towel.
2. Trim the bottom of each Brussels sprout's hard stem with a sharp knife and cut each Brussels sprout in half lengthwise, from tip to trimmed end.
3. In a medium mixing dish, place the Brussel sprouts. Season with garlic powder, salt, and pepper. Then, drizzle with olive oil and balsamic vinegar.
4. Toss them in the seasoning until they're evenly covered. It's best to do this using your hands.
5. Press either "Zone 1" or "Zone 2" and then rotate the knob to select "Bake".
6. Set the temperature to 200 degrees C, and then set the time for 5 minutes to preheat.
7. After preheating, arrange them into the basket.
8. Slide the basket into the Air Fryer and set the time for 15 minutes.
9. After cooking time is completed, transfer onto serving plates and serve.

Serving Suggestions: Serve with lemon wedges.
Variation Tip: You can also sprinkle parsley on top.
Nutritional Information per Serving:
Calories: 85 | Fat: 4g | Sat Fat: 1g | Carbohydrates: 11g | Fibre: 4g | Sugar: 3g | Protein: 4g

Air Fryer Red Potato Bites

Preparation Time: 10 minutes | Cooking Time: 20 minutes | Servings: 6

Ingredients:

900g red potatoes
2 tablespoons olive oil
½ teaspoon salt
¼ teaspoon pepper

Preparation:

1. Wash the potatoes and chop them into 1 cm bite-size pieces.
2. In a big colander, place the cut potatoes and run them under cold water for about 5 minutes, turning them a few times.
3. Place the potatoes on a few paper towels to absorb any excess moisture.
4. Place the potatoes in a mixing bowl. To coat, toss with the oil and seasonings.
5. Press your chosen zone - "Zone 1" or "Zone 2" and then rotate the knob to select "Air Fryer".
6. Set the temperature to 190 degrees C, and then set the time for 5 minutes to preheat.
7. After preheating, arrange potatoes into the basket of each zone.
8. Slide the baskets into Air Fryer and set the time for 15 minutes.
9. While cooking, toss the potato pieces once halfway through.
10. After cooking time is completed, transfer the fries onto serving plates and serve.

Serving Suggestions: Sprinkle parsley on top.
Variation Tip: You can use any oil.
Nutritional Information per Serving:
Calories: 147 | Fat: 5g | Sat Fat: 1g | Carbohydrates: 24g | Fibre: 3g | Sugar: 2g | Protein: 3g

Garlic Cheese Asparagus

Preparation Time: 5 minutes | Cooking Time: 8 minutes | Servings: 4

Ingredients:

1 bundle asparagus
1 teaspoon olive oil
⅛ teaspoon garlic salt
1 tablespoon Parmesan cheese
Pepper, to taste

Preparation:

1. Clean the asparagus and dry it. To remove the woody stalks, cut 2.5cm off the bottom.
2. Place asparagus in a single layer in the air fryer and spray with oil.
3. On top of the asparagus, evenly sprinkle garlic salt. Season with salt and pepper, then sprinkle with Parmesan cheese.
4. Press either "Zone 1" or "Zone 2" and then rotate the knob to select "Air Fryer".
5. Set the temperature to 200 degrees C, and then set the time for 5 minutes to preheat.
6. After preheating, arrange them into the basket.
7. Slide the basket into the Air Fryer and set the time for 8 minutes.
8. After cooking time is completed, transfer onto serving plates and serve.

Serving Suggestions: Sprinkle parsley on top.
Variation Tip: You can use powdered or grated cheese.
Nutritional Information per Serving:
Calories: 18 | Fat: 2g | Sat Fat: 9g | Carbohydrates: 1g | Fibre: 0g | Sugar: 0g | Protein: 1g

Crispy Cheese Aubergine

Preparation Time: 10 minutes | Cooking Time: 10 minutes | Servings: 4

Ingredients:

1 aubergine
1 egg, whisked
25g Italian breadcrumbs
25g grated Parmesan cheese
½ teaspoon garlic powder
½ teaspoon dried basil
55g shredded mozzarella cheese

Preparation:

1. Place the aubergine slices on a baking sheet and cut them into 2.5cm thick disks. Salt the aubergine and set it aside for at least 15 minutes.
2. In one bowl, beat the egg; in another, combine the breadcrumbs, Parmesan cheese, garlic powder, and basil.
3. Dip each aubergine slice into the egg, then into the breadcrumb mixture, ensuring each piece is completely covered.
4. Press either "Zone 1" and "Zone 2" and then rotate the knob to select "Air Fryer".
5. Set the temperature to 185 degrees C, and then set the time for 5 minutes to preheat.
6. After preheating, arrange them into the basket.
7. Slide the basket into the Air Fryer and set the time for 10 minutes.
8. After cooking time is completed, transfer onto serving plates and top with mozzarella cheese and serve.

Serving Suggestions: Serve with marinara sauce.
Variation Tip: You can use any bread crumbs.
Nutritional Information per Serving:
Calories: 173 | Fat: 6g | Sat Fat: 3g | Carbohydrates: 22g | Fibre: 4g | Sugar: 5g | Protein: 9g

Cheesy Bacon Stuffed Mushrooms

Preparation Time: 10 minutes | Cooking Time: 15 minutes | Servings: 4

Ingredients:

9 baby Bella mushrooms
100g cream cheese
25g bacon crumbles
24g Parmesan cheese
Salt and pepper to taste

Preparation:

1. Remove the stems from the baby Bella mushrooms.
2. Cut the stems into dice.
3. Combine cream cheese, bacon crumbles, Parmesan cheese, and diced mushroom stem in a mixing bowl.
4. Stuff the mixture into the mushrooms. Season with salt and pepper.
5. Press your chosen zone - "Zone 1" or "Zone 2" and then rotate the knob to select "Air Fry".
6. Set the temperature to 195 degrees C, and then set the time for 5 minutes to preheat.
7. After preheating, spray the Air-Fryer basket of each zone with cooking spray, and arrange them.
8. Slide the basket into the Air Fryer and set the time for 8 minutes.
9. After cooking time is completed, place them on a serving plate and serve.

Serving Suggestions: Sprinkle parsley on top.
Variation Tip: You can use any cheese.
Nutritional Information per Serving:
Calories: 135 | Fat: 11g | Sat Fat: 6g | Carbohydrates: 0.8g | Fibre: 0g | Sugar: 0.1g | Protein: 5g

Baked Garlicky Mushrooms

Preparation Time: 10 minutes | Cooking Time: 10 minutes | Servings: 2

▶ **Ingredients:**

200g Bella mushroom cut into half
1 tablespoon olive oil
½ teaspoon garlic powder
1 teaspoon soy sauce
Salt and pepper, to taste

▶ **Preparation:**

1. To begin, clean the mushrooms. To clean them, use a moist kitchen towel to wipe them down.
2. Avoid getting wet or rushing in the water. Remove the stems from the mushrooms and cut them in half.
3. Season mushrooms with garlic powder, salt, and pepper, and toss with olive oil and soy sauce.
4. Press either "Zone 1" or "Zone 2" and then rotate the knob to select "Bake".
5. Set the temperature to 200 degrees C and then set the time for 5 minutes to preheat.
6. After preheating, arrange them into the basket.
7. Slide the basket into the Air Fryer and set the time for 10 minutes.
8. After cooking time is completed, transfer onto serving plates and serve.

Serving Suggestions: Serve with lemon wedges.
Variation Tip: You can also sprinkle parsley on top.
Nutritional Information per Serving:
Calories: 92 | Fat: 7g | Sat Fat: 1g | Carbohydrates: 6g | Fibre: 1g | Sugar: 2g | Protein: 3g

Buttery Squash slices

Preparation Time: 15 minutes | Cooking Time: 15 minutes | Servings: 6

▶ **Ingredients:**

2 medium butternut squash
130g packed brown sugar
115g butter, softened

▶ **Preparation:**

1. Cut squash in half lengthwise and remove the seeds. Cut each half into 1cm slices.
2. Press your chosen zone - "Zone 1" or "Zone 2" and then rotate the knob to select "Air Fry".
3. Set the temperature to 200 degrees C, and then set the time for 5 minutes to preheat.
4. After preheating, spray the Air-Fryer basket of each zone with cooking spray and place slices in a single layer.
5. Slide the basket into the Air Fryer and set the time for 5 minutes.
6. Carefully turn them and cook for 5 more minutes.
7. Combine sugar and butter; spread over squash and cook 3 minutes longer.
8. After cooking time is completed, serve avocado slices in tortillas with kale mix, tomato, and additional minced coriander and place them on a serving plate and serve.

Serving Suggestions: Sprinkle parsley on top.
Variation Tip: You can add more chopped veggies.
Nutritional Information per Serving:
Calories: 320 | Fat: 16g | Sat Fat: 10g | Carbohydrates: 48g | Fibre: 3g | Sugar: 29g | Protein: 2g

Healthy Beans & Veggie Burgers

Preparation Time: 15 minutes | Cooking Time: 15 minutes | Servings: 8

Ingredients:

- 330g cooked black beans
- 560g boiled potatoes, peeled and mashed
- 60g fresh spinach, chopped
- 175g fresh mushrooms, chopped
- 4 teaspoons Chile lime seasoning
- Olive oil cooking spray

Preparation:

1. In a large bowl, add the beans, potatoes, spinach, mushrooms, and seasoning and with your hands, mix until well combined.
2. Make 8 equal-sized patties from the mixture.
3. Spray the patties with cooking spray evenly.
4. Grease basket of Ninja Foodi 2-Basket Air Fryer.
5. Press your chosen zone - "Zone 1" or "Zone 2" and then rotate the knob to select "Air Fry".
6. Set the temperature to 185 degrees C and then set the time for 5 minutes to preheat.
7. After preheating, arrange 4 patties into the basket of each zone.
8. Slide the basket into the Air Fryer and set the time for 12 minutes.
9. After cooking time is completed, remove the patties from Air Fryer.
10. Serve hot.

Serving Suggestions: Serve with fresh greens.
Variation Tip: Feel free to use seasoning of your choice.
Nutritional Information per Serving:
Calories: 113 | Fat: 0.4g | Sat Fat: 0g | Carbohydrates: 23.1g | Fibre: 6.2g | Sugar: 1.7g | Protein: 6g

Chili Butternut Squash

Preparation Time: 10 minutes | Cooking Time: 20 minutes | Servings: 2

Ingredients:

- 1 small butternut squash, peeled and cut into 1.5cm cubes
- 1 tablespoon extra-virgin olive oil
- ½ teaspoon garlic powder
- ½ teaspoon salt
- ⅛ teaspoon freshly ground black pepper
- 1 teaspoon chili flakes

Preparation:

1. For consistent and speedy cooking, peel and cut the butternut squash into 1.5cm chunks.
2. Place the butternut squash in a mixing dish. Season with garlic powder, salt, chili flakes, and pepper and drizzle with olive oil.
3. Toss them well so that the spice is evenly distributed.
4. Press either "Zone 1" or "Zone 2" and then rotate the knob to select "Bake".
5. Set the temperature to 200 degrees C, and then set the time for 5 minutes to preheat.
6. After preheating, arrange them into the basket,
7. Slide the basket into the Air Fryer and set the time for 25 minutes.
8. After cooking time is completed, transfer onto serving plates and serve.

Serving Suggestions: Serve with lemon wedges.
Variation Tip: You can also sprinkle parsley on top.
Nutritional Information per Serving:
Calories: 148 | Fat: 7g | Sat Fat: 1g | Carbohydrates: 22g | Fibre: 4g | Sugar: 4g | Protein: 2g

Crispy Herb Potatoes

Preparation Time: 10 minutes | Cooking Time: 20 minutes | Servings: 2

Ingredients:

Cajun Mayonnaise Dressing

4 tablespoons mayonnaise
1 teaspoon garlic powder
½ teaspoon dried oregano
½ teaspoon dried thyme
½ teaspoon ground black pepper
1 teaspoon red chili powder
1 teaspoon tomato ketchup
Salt, to taste
1-2 teaspoons of milk (optional)

Crispy Potatoes:

10-12 baby potatoes
2 tablespoons corn flour
Salt, to taste
2 tablespoons onions finely chopped

Preparation:

1. To begin, in a mixing bowl, combine the mayonnaise, tomato ketchup, and all of the spices listed in the Cajun Mayonnaise Dressing ingredients section.
2. Set Aside. If the dressing is too thick, add 1-2 teaspoons of milk. To achieve the desired consistency, I frequently add milk.
3. Scrub the tiny potatoes to remove any dirt and cook for 7 minutes in the microwave.
4. Mix in a little corn flour with the potatoes until lightly coated on both sides.
5. Press your chosen zone - "Zone 1" or "Zone 2" and then rotate the knob to select "Air Fryer".
6. Set the temperature to 200 degrees C, and then set the time for 5 minutes to preheat.
7. After preheating, arrange them into the basket of each zone.
8. Slide the baskets into Air Fryer and set the time for 15 minutes.
9. After cooking time is completed, transfer onto serving plates. Add Cajun Mayonnaise Dressing on each potato and finely chopped onions, and serve.

Serving Suggestions: Serve with coriander on top.
Variation Tip: You can use spices of your choice.
Nutritional Information per Serving:
Calories: 253 | Fat: 8g | Sat Fat: 2g | Carbohydrates: 43g | Fibre: 5g | Sugar: 2g | Protein: 5g

Crispy Courgette Fries

Preparation Time: 25 minutes | Cooking Time: 12 minutes | Servings: 4

Ingredients:

65g flour
2 eggs, beaten
100g seasoned breadcrumbs
Salt and freshly ground
black pepper
1 large courgette, cut into sticks
Olive oil

Preparation:

1. Make the courgette fries first. Season the flour generously with salt and freshly ground black pepper in the first shallow dish.
2. In the second shallow dish, beat the eggs. Combine the breadcrumbs, salt, and pepper in the third shallow dish.
3. Dredge the courgette sticks by first coating them in flour, then dipping them in eggs to coat them, and finally tossing them in breadcrumbs.
4. Shake the breadcrumbs into the dish and gently pat the crumbs into the courgette sticks with your palms to ensure even coverage.
5. Press either "Zone 1" or "Zone 2" and then rotate the knob to select "Air Fryer".
6. Set the temperature to 200 degrees C, and then set the time for 5 minutes to preheat.
7. After preheating, arrange them into the basket.
8. Slide the basket into the Air Fryer and set the time for 12 minutes. Turning the fries halfway through the cooking time.
9. After cooking time is completed, transfer onto serving plates and serve.

Serving Suggestions: Serve with garlic sauce.
Variation Tip: You can use any crumbs.
Nutritional Information per Serving:
Calories: 464 | Fat: 5g | Sat Fat: 5g | Carbohydrates: 34g | Fibre: 2g | Sugar: 3g | Protein: 9g

Vegetable Stuffed Peppers

Preparation Time: 15 minutes | Cooking Time: 25 minutes | Servings: 6

Ingredients:

- 6 large peppers
- 1 bread roll, finely chopped
- 130g carrot, peeled and finely chopped
- 1 onion, finely chopped
- 1 potato, peeled and finely chopped
- 85g fresh peas, shelled
- 2 garlic cloves, minced
- 2 teaspoons fresh parsley, chopped
- Salt and ground black pepper, as required
- 35g cheddar cheese, grated

Preparation:

1. Remove the top of each pepper and discard the seeds.
2. Finely chop the pepper tops.
3. In a bowl, place pepper tops, bread loaf, vegetables, garlic, parsley, salt and black pepper and mix well.
4. Stuff each pepper with the vegetable mixture.
5. Grease basket of Ninja Foodi 2-Basket Air Fryer.
6. Press your chosen zone - "Zone 1" or "Zone 2" and then rotate the knob to select "Air Fry".
7. Set the temperature to 175 degrees C and then set the time for 5 minutes to preheat.
8. After preheating, arrange 3 peppers into the basket of each zone.
9. Slide the basket into the Air Fryer and set the time for 25 minutes.
10. After 20 minutes, sprinkle each pepper with cheddar cheese.
11. After cooking time is completed, remove the peppers from Air Fryer and serve hot.

Serving Suggestions: Serve with the garnishing of fresh herbs.
Variation Tip: You can use multi-coloured peppers.
Calories: 123 | Fat: 2.7g | Sat Fat: 1.3g | Carbohydrates: 21.7g | Fibre: 3.7g | Sugar: 8.7g | Protein: 4.8g

Crispy Cheese Garlic Broccoli

Preparation Time: 7 minutes | Cooking Time: 5 minutes | Servings: 2

Ingredients:

- 225g broccoli washed, dried, and cut into bite-sized pieces
- 1 tablespoon olive oil
- 1 tablespoon parmesan cheese grated
- 1 clove garlic minced
- Salt & pepper, to taste

Preparation:

1. Combine the broccoli, olive oil, cheese, and garlic in a container with a cover and shake until equally coated.
2. Any remaining cheese should be pressed into the broccoli florets. To taste, season with salt and pepper.
3. Press either "Zone 1" or "Zone 2" and then rotate the knob to select "Air Fryer".
4. Set the temperature to 200 degrees C, and then set the time for 5 minutes to preheat.
5. After preheating, arrange them into the basket.
6. Slide the basket into the Air Fryer and set the time for 5 minutes.
7. After cooking time is completed, transfer onto serving plates and serve.

Serving Suggestions: Serve with coriander on top.
Variation Tip: You can use any cheese.
Nutritional Information per Serving:
Calories: 112 | Fat: 8g | Sat Fat: 1g | Carbohydrates: 8g | Fibre: 3g | Sugar: 2g | Protein: 4g

Air Fryer Rice with Peas & Carrots

Preparation Time: 15 minutes | Cooking Time: 18 minutes | Servings: 8

Ingredients:

- 500g cooked white rice
- 1 tablespoon vegetable oil
- 2 teaspoons sesame oil, toasted and divided
- 1 tablespoon water
- Salt and ground white pepper, as required
- 1 large egg, lightly beaten
- 85g frozen peas, thawed
- 55g frozen carrots, thawed
- 1 teaspoon Sriracha sauce
- 1 teaspoon soy sauce
- ½ teaspoon of toasted sesame seeds

Preparation:

1. In a large bowl, add the rice, oil, 1 teaspoon of sesame oil, water, salt, and white pepper and mix well.
2. Divide the rice mixture into 2 lightly greased baking pans.
3. Press "Zone 1" and "Zone 2" of Ninja Foodi 2-Basket Air Fryer and then rotate the knob for each zone to select "Air Fry".
4. Set the temperature to 195 degrees C and then set the time for 5 minutes to preheat.
5. After preheating, arrange 1 baking pan into the basket of each zone.
6. Slide the basket into the Air Fryer and set the time for 18 minutes.
7. While cooking, stir the rice mixture once after 5 minutes.
8. After 12 minutes of cooking, place the beaten egg over rice.
9. After 15 minutes of cooking, stir in the peas and carrots into each pan.
10. Meanwhile, in a bowl, mix together soy sauce, Sriracha sauce, sesame seeds and the remaining sesame oil.
11. After cooking time is completed, remove the baking pans from Air Fryer and transfer the rice mixture into a serving bowl.
12. Drizzle with the sauce and serve.

Serving Suggestions: Serve with the drizzling of lemon juice.
Variation Tip: You can use veggies of your choice.
Nutritional Information per Serving:
Calories: 438 | Fat: 8.6g | Sat Fat: 1.7g | Carbohydrates: 78g | Fibre: 2.7g | Sugar: 1.9g | Protein: 9.5g

Tofu in Ginger Orange Sauce

Preparation Time: 15 minutes | Cooking Time: 10 minutes | Servings: 4

Ingredients:

For Tofu:
- 455g extra-firm tofu, pressed, drained and cubed
- 1 tablespoon cornflour
- 1 tablespoon tamari

For Sauce:
- 120ml water
- 80ml fresh orange juice
- 1 tablespoon maple syrup
- 1 teaspoon orange zest, grated
- 1 teaspoon garlic, minced
- 1 teaspoon fresh ginger, minced
- 2 teaspoons cornflour
- ¼ teaspoon red pepper flakes, crushed

Preparation:

1. In a bowl, add the tofu, cornflour, and tamari and toss to coat well.
2. Set the tofu aside to marinate for at least 15 minutes.
3. Grease basket of Ninja Foodi 2-Basket Air Fryer.
4. Press either "Zone 1" or "Zone 2" and then rotate the knob to select "Air Fry".
5. Set the temperature to 200 degrees C, and then set the time for 5 minutes to preheat.
6. After preheating, arrange tofu cubes into the basket.
7. Slide basket into Air Fryer and set the time for 10 minutes.
8. Flip the tofu cubes once halfway through.
9. Meanwhile, for the sauce: in a small pan, add all the ingredients over medium-high heat and bring to a boil, stirring continuously.
10. Remove from heat and transfer the sauce into a serving bowl.
11. After cooking time is completed, remove the tofu cubes from Air Fryer.
12. Place the tofu cubes into the bowl with sauce and gently stir to combine.
13. Serve immediately.

Serving Suggestions: Serve with the garnishing of spring onion greens.
Variation Tip: For best result, use freshly squeezed orange juice.
Nutritional Information per Serving:
Calories: 147 | Fat: 6.7g | Sat Fat: 0.6g | Carbohydrates: 12.7g | Fibre: 0.7g | Sugar: 6.7g | Protein: 12.1g

Spicy Buttered Cauliflower

Preparation Time: 15 minutes | Cooking Time: 15 minutes | Servings: 8

▶ **Ingredients:**

- 900g cauliflower head, cut into florets
- 2 tablespoons butter, melted
- 1 teaspoon red pepper flakes, crushed
- Salt and ground black pepper, as required

▶ **Preparation:**

1. Grease basket of Ninja Foodi 2-Basket Air Fryer.
2. Press your chosen zone - "Zone 1" or "Zone 2" and then rotate the knob to select "Air Fry".
3. Set the temperature to 200 degrees C and then set the time for 5 minutes to preheat.
4. In a bowl, add all the ingredients and toss to coat well.
5. After preheating, arrange the cauliflower florets into the basket of each zone.
6. Slide the basket into the Air Fryer and set the time for 15 minutes.
7. After cooking time is completed, remove the cauliflower florets from Air Fryer and serve hot.

Serving Suggestions: Serve with the drizzling of lemon juice.
Variation Tip: You can use spices of your choice.
Nutritional Information per Serving:
Calories: 55 | Fat: 3g | Sat Fat: 1.9g | Carbohydrates: 6.1g | Fibre: 2.9g | Sugar: 2.7g | Protein: 2.3g

Simple Buttered Green Beans

Preparation Time: 10 minutes | Cooking Time: 10 minutes | Servings: 6

▶ **Ingredients:**

- 675g green beans, trimmed
- 4 tablespoons butter, melted
- Salt and ground black pepper, as required

▶ **Preparation:**

1. Grease basket of Ninja Foodi 2-Basket Air Fryer.
2. Press your chosen zone - "Zone 1" or "Zone 2" and then rotate the knob to select "Air Fry".
3. Set the temperature to 200 degrees C and then set the time for 5 minutes to preheat.
4. In a bowl, add all the ingredients and toss to coat well.
5. After preheating, arrange the green beans into the basket of each zone.
6. Slide the basket into the Air Fryer and set the time for 10 minutes.
7. While cooking, flip the green beans once halfway through.
8. After cooking time is completed, remove the green beans from Air Fryer and serve hot.

Serving Suggestions: Serve with lemon wedges.
Variation Tip: Use fresh green beans.
Nutritional Information per Serving:
Calories: 103 | Fat: 7.8g | Sat Fat: 4.9g | Carbohydrates: 8.1g | Fibre: 3.9g | Sugar: 1.6g | Protein: 2.1g

Honey Glazed Carrots

Preparation Time: 15 minutes | Cooking Time: 12 minutes | Servings: 6

Ingredients:

440g carrots, peeled and cut into large chunks
2 tablespoons olive oil
2 tablespoons honey
1 tablespoon fresh thyme, chopped finely
Salt and ground black pepper, as required

Preparation:

1. Grease basket of Ninja Foodi 2-Basket Air Fryer.
2. Press your chosen zone - "Zone 1" or "Zone 2" and then rotate the knob to select "Air Fry".
3. Set the temperature to 200 degrees C and then set the time for 5 minutes to preheat.
4. In a bowl, place all ingredients and toss to coat well.
5. After preheating, arrange the carrot chunks into the basket of each zone.
6. Slide the basket into the Air Fryer and set the time for 12 minutes.
7. After cooking time is completed, remove carrot chunks from Air Fryer.
8. Cut each carrot chunks into half and serve hot.

Serving Suggestions: Serve with the topping of fresh herbs.
Variation Tip: Honey can be replaced with maple syrup.
Nutritional Information per Serving:
Calories: 93 | Fat: 4.7g | Sat Fat: 0.7g | Carbohydrates: 13.3g | Fibre: 2g | Sugar: 9.4g | Protein: 0.7g

Classic Hasselback Potatoes

Preparation Time: 10 minutes | Cooking Time: 30 minutes | Servings: 8

Ingredients:

8 potatoes
4 tablespoons olive oil

Preparation:

1. With a sharp knife, cut slits along each potato the short way about ½ cm apart, making sure slices should stay connected at the bottom.
2. Grease basket of Ninja Foodi 2-Basket Air Fryer.
3. Press your chosen zone - "Zone 1" or "Zone 2" and then rotate the knob to select "Air Fry".
4. Set the temperature to 180 degrees C and then set the time for 5 minutes to preheat.
5. After preheating, arrange 4 potatoes into the basket of each zone.
6. Slide the basket into the Air Fryer and set the time for 30 minutes.
7. After 15 minutes of cooking, coat the potatoes with oil.
8. After cooking time is completed, remove the baking pan of potatoes from Air Fryer and serve immediately.

Serving Suggestions: Serve with the topping of parmesan cheese.
Variation Tip: Use equal-sized potatoes.
Nutritional Information per Serving:
Calories: 207 | Fat: 7.2g | Sat Fat: 1.1g | Carbohydrates: 33.5g | Fibre: 5.1g | Sugar: 2.5g | Protein: 3.6g

Spiced Butter Courgette

Preparation Time: 10 minutes | Cooking Time: 15 minutes | Servings: 6

Ingredients:

- 675g courgettes, sliced
- 2 tablespoons butter, melted
- ½ teaspoon dried rosemary, crushed
- ½ teaspoon ground cumin
- ½ teaspoon ground coriander
- ½ teaspoon cayenne pepper
- Salt and ground black pepper, as required

Preparation:

1. Grease basket of Ninja Foodi 2-Basket Air Fryer.
2. Press your chosen zone - "Zone 1" or "Zone 2" and then rotate the knob to select "Air Fry".
3. Set the temperature to 200 degrees C and then set the time for 5 minutes to preheat.
4. In a large bowl, add all ingredients and mix well.
5. After preheating, arrange the courgette slices into the basket of each zone.
6. Slide the basket into the Air Fryer and set the time for 15 minutes.
7. After cooking time is completed, remove the squash chunks from Air Fryer.
8. Transfer the courgette slices onto a platter and serve hot.

Serving Suggestions: Serve with the drizzling of lemon juice.

Variation Tip: You can use yellow squash instead of courgette too.

Nutritional Information per Serving:

Calories: 54 | Fat: 4.1g | Sat Fat: 25g | Carbohydrates: 4g | Fibre: 1.4g | Sugar: 2g | Protein: 1.5g

Easy Balsamic Asparagus

Preparation Time: 10 minutes | Cooking Time: 6 minutes | Servings: 6

Ingredients:

- 675g asparagus
- 4 tablespoons olive oil
- 3 tablespoon balsamic vinegar
- Salt and ground black pepper, as required

Preparation:

1. Grease basket of Ninja Foodi 2-Basket Air Fryer.
2. Press your chosen zone - "Zone 1" or "Zone 2" and then rotate the knob to select "Air Fry".
3. Set the temperature to 200 degrees C and then set the time for 5 minutes to preheat.
4. In a bowl, mix together the asparagus, oil, vinegar, salt, and black pepper.
5. After preheating, arrange the asparagus into the basket of each zone.
6. Slide the basket into the Air Fryer and set the time for 6 minutes.
7. After cooking time is completed, remove the asparagus from Air Fryer and serve hot.

Serving Suggestions: Serve with the topping of Parmesan cheese.

Variation Tip: You can use butter instead of oil.

Nutritional Information per Serving:

Calories: 104 | Fat: 9.5g | Sat Fat: 1.4g | Carbohydrates: 4.5g | Fibre: 2.4g | Sugar: 2.2g | Protein: 2.5g

Chapter 4 Fish and Seafood Recipes

Cheese Crumb-Topped Sole

Preparation Time: 10 minutes | Cooking Time: 10 minutes | Servings: 4

Ingredients:

3 tablespoons mayonnaise
3 tablespoons grated Parmesan cheese, divided
2 teaspoons mustard seed
¼ teaspoon pepper
4 sole fillets
100g soft bread crumbs
1 green onion, finely chopped
½ teaspoon ground mustard
2 teaspoons butter, melted
Cooking spray

Preparation:

1. Mix mayonnaise, 2 tablespoons cheese, mustard seed and pepper; spread over tops of fillets.
2. Press your chosen zone - "Zone 1" or "Zone 2" and then rotate the knob to select "Air Fry".
3. Set the temperature to 190 degrees C, and then set the time for 5 minutes to preheat.
4. After preheating, spray the Air-Fryer basket of each zone with cooking spray, arrange fish in a single layer, and spray with cooking spray.
5. Slide the basket into the Air Fryer and set the time for 5 minutes.
6. Meanwhile, combine bread crumbs, onion, crushed mustard, and the remaining 1 tablespoon of cheese in a small bowl; whisk in butter.
7. Spritz top with cooking spray and spoon over fillets, carefully patting to adhere and cook for 5 more minutes.
8. After cooking time is completed, place them on a serving plate and serve.

Serving Suggestions: Serve with any sauce.
Variation Tip: You can use mustard sauce instead of mustard seeds.
Nutritional Information per Serving:
Calories: 233 | Fat: 11g | Sat Fat: 3g | Carbohydrates: 8g | Fibre: 1g | Sugar: 1g | Protein: 24g

Cheese Prawn Salad

Preparation Time: 15 minutes | Cooking Time: 5 minutes | Servings: 4

Ingredients:

2 romaine hearts, coarsely chopped
150g cherry tomatoes, halved
25g shredded Parmesan cheese
65g plain flour
¾ teaspoon salt
½ teaspoon pepper
455g uncooked prawns, peeled and deveined
Cooking spray
120g Creamy Caesar Salad Dressing

Preparation:

1. Combine romaine hearts, tomatoes, and cheese in a large mixing basin; chill until ready to serve.
2. Combine flour, salt, and pepper in a small bowl. Toss in a few pieces of prawn at a time, tossing to coat; brush off excess.
3. Press your chosen zone - "Zone 1" or "Zone 2" and then rotate the knob to select "Air Fry".
4. Set the temperature to 190 degrees C, and then set the time for 5 minutes to preheat.
5. After preheating, spray the Air-Fryer basket of each zone with cooking spray, arrange prawns in a single layer, and spritz them with cooking spray.
6. Slide the basket into the Air Fryer and set the time for 4 minutes.
7. Carefully turn them and cook 4 minutes longer.
8. After cooking time is completed, toss the romaine mixture with the dressing to coat it, put prawns on top, and place them on a serving plate and serve.

Serving Suggestions: Serve lemon juice on top.
Variation Tip: You can use any salad dressing.
Nutritional Information per Serving:
Calories: 313 | Fat: 21g | Sat Fat: 4g | Carbohydrates: 8g | Fibre: 2g | Sugar: 2g | Protein: 23g

Coconut Prawns in Buns

Preparation Time: 35 minutes | Cooking Time: 10 minutes | Servings: 4

Ingredients:

120g mayonnaise
1 tablespoon Creole mustard
1 tablespoon chopped dill
pickles
1 tablespoon minced shallot
1½ teaspoons lemon juice

Coconut Prawns:

125g plain flour
½ teaspoon sea salt
½ teaspoon garlic powder
½ teaspoon pepper
¼ teaspoon cayenne pepper
1 large egg
120ml low fat milk
1 teaspoon hot pepper sauce
140g sweetened shredded coconut
455g uncooked prawns, peeled and deveined
Cooking spray
4 hoagie buns, split
110g shredded lettuce
1 medium tomato, thinly sliced

Preparation:

1. Combine the first 5 ingredients for remoulade in a small bowl. Refrigerate until ready to serve, covered.
2. Combine flour, herbs, sea salt, garlic powder, and pepper in a bowl.
3. Whisk the egg, milk, and hot pepper sauce in a separate bowl. In a third bowl, place the coconut.
4. Coat both sides of the prawn with flour and shake off excess. Dip in the egg mixture, then in the coconut, patting it down to help it stick.
5. Press your chosen zone - "Zone 1" or "Zone 2" and then rotate the knob to select "Air Fry".
6. Set the temperature to 190 degrees C, and then set the time for 5 minutes to preheat.
7. After preheating, spray the Air-Fryer basket of each zone with cooking spray, arrange prawns in a single layer, and spritz them with cooking spray.
8. Slide the basket into the Air Fryer and set the time for 5 minutes.
9. Carefully turn them and cook 5 minutes longer.
10. After cooking time is completed, spread the cut side of the buns with mayo. Top with prawn, lettuce and tomato and place them on a serving plate and serve.

Serving Suggestions: Serve with any sauce.
Variation Tip: You can also add cayenne pepper.
Nutritional Information per Serving:
Calories: 716 | Fat: 40g | Sat Fat: 16g | Carbohydrates: 60g | Fibre: 4g | Sugar: 23g | Protein: 31g

Prawns in Tacos with Coleslaw

Preparation Time: 20 minutes | Cooking Time: 10 minutes | Servings: 4

Ingredients:

140g coleslaw mix
5g minced fresh coriander
2 tablespoons lime juice
2 tablespoons honey
¼ teaspoon salt
2 large eggs
2 tablespoons low-fat milk
65g plain flour
110g panko bread crumbs
1 tablespoon ground cumin
1 tablespoon garlic powder
455g uncooked prawns, peeled
Cooking spray
8 corn tortillas
1 medium ripe avocado, peeled and sliced

Preparation:

1. Toss coleslaw mix, coriander, lime juice, honey, and salt in a small bowl to coat. Set aside.
2. Whisk the eggs and milk together in a small bowl. In a separate shallow bowl, place the flour.
3. Combine panko, cumin, and garlic powder in a third shallow bowl. Coat both sides of the prawns with flour and shake off excess.
4. Dip in the egg mixture, then in the panko mixture, patting to ensure that the coating sticks.
5. Press your chosen zone - "Zone 1" or "Zone 2" and then rotate the knob to select "Air Fry".
6. Set the temperature to 190 degrees C, and then set the time for 5 minutes to preheat.
7. After preheating, spray the Air-Fryer basket of each zone with cooking spray, arrange prawns in a single layer, and spritz them with cooking spray.
8. Slide the basket into the Air Fryer and set the time for 5 minutes.
9. Carefully turn them and cook 5 minutes longer.
10. After cooking time is completed, place prawns in tortillas with coleslaw mix and avocado, place them on a serving plate and serve.

Serving Suggestions: Serve lemon juice on top.
Variation Tip: You can also add sliced jalapeno pepper.
Nutritional Information per Serving:
Calories: 456 | Fat: 12g | Sat Fat: 2g | Carbohydrates: 58g | Fibre: 8g | Sugar: 11g | Protein: 29g

Crispy Oysters

Preparation Time: 10 minutes | Cooking Time: 10 minutes | Servings: 2

Ingredients:

- 455g raw, shucked oysters
- 65g plain flour
- 1 teaspoon Cajun seasoning
- ½ teaspoon salt
- ¼ teaspoon black pepper
- 1 large egg
- 1 tablespoon milk
- 165g panko breadcrumbs
- Melted garlic butter for serving

Preparation:

1. Drain the oysters in a colander after shucking and rinsing them. Using paper towels, pat the shucked oysters dry.
2. Mix the flour, Cajun spice, salt, and pepper in a small bowl.
3. Whisk the egg and milk together in a separate bowl. Add the panko breadcrumbs to a third bowl.
4. Dip the oysters in the flour, dip them in the egg, and roll them in the breadcrumbs.
5. Press your chosen zone - "Zone 1" or "Zone 2" and then rotate the knob to select "Air Fry".
6. Set the temperature to 175 degrees C, and then set the time for 5 minutes to preheat.
7. After preheating, spray the Air-Fryer basket of each zone with cooking spray, arrange oysters in a single layer, and spritz them with cooking spray.
8. Slide the basket into the Air Fryer and set the time for 4 minutes.
9. Carefully turn them and cook 4 minutes longer.
10. After cooking time is completed, let tuna steaks rest for a minute or two, then sliced, place them on a serving plate and serve.

Serving Suggestions: Serve with lemon wedges.
Variation Tip: You can also sprinkle sesame seeds on top.
Nutritional Information per Serving:
Calories: 892 | Fat: 22g | Sat Fat: 7g | Carbohydrates: 109g | Fibre: 6g | Sugar: 6g | Protein: 61g

Honey Glazed Tuna Steaks

Preparation Time: 15 minutes | Cooking Time: 6 minutes | Servings: 2

Ingredients:

- 2 boneless and skinless yellowfin tuna steaks
- 60ml soy sauce
- 2 teaspoons honey
- 1 teaspoon grated ginger
- 1 teaspoon sesame oil
- ½ teaspoon rice vinegar

Preparation:

1. Combine the grated ginger, soy sauce, honey, sesame oil, and rice vinegar in a large mixing bowl.
2. Place the tuna steaks in the marinade and leave to marinate in the fridge for 20-30 minutes, covered.
3. Press your chosen zone - "Zone 1" or "Zone 2" and then rotate the knob to select "Air Fry".
4. Set the temperature to 195 degrees C, and then set the time for 5 minutes to preheat.
5. After preheating, spray the Air-Fryer basket of each zone with cooking spray, arrange tuna in a single layer, and spritz them with cooking spray.
6. Slide the basket into the Air Fryer and set the time for 4 minutes.
7. Carefully turn them and cook 2 minutes longer.
8. After cooking time is completed, let tuna steaks rest for a minute or two, then sliced, place them on a serving plate and serve.

Serving Suggestions: Sprinkle green onions on top.
Variation Tip: You can also sprinkle sesame seeds on top.
Nutritional Information per Serving:
Calories: 422 | Fat: 23g | Sat Fat: 8g | Carbohydrates: 8g | Fibre: 0g | Sugar: 6g | Protein: 44g

Cheese-Crusted Tuna Patties

Preparation Time: 10 minutes | Cooking Time: 10 minutes | Servings: 3

Ingredients:

Tuna Patties

- 1 tablespoon butter
- 80g onion chopped
- ½ red pepper chopped
- 1 teaspoon minced garlic
- 2 (175g) cans of tuna fish, drained
- 1 tablespoon lime juice
- 15g fresh parsley chopped
- 3 tablespoons of parmesan cheese grated
- ½ teaspoon oregano
- ¼ teaspoon salt
- Black pepper to taste
- 55g panko crumbs
- 2 eggs whisked

Crumb Coating

- 55g panko crumbs
- 25g parmesan cheese
- Cooking spray

Preparation:

1. In a frying pan, heat the oil and butter over medium-high heat.
2. Sauté for 5-7 minutes with the onions, red pepper, and garlic.
3. Drain tuna cans thoroughly. Fill a medium mixing bowl halfway with the mixture. Lime juice should be poured over the tuna.
4. Place sautéed vegetables in a mixing bowl. Combine parsley and cheese in a mixing bowl.
5. Add oregano, salt, and pepper to taste. Add the panko crumbs and mix well.
6. Mix in the eggs until the mixture forms a beautiful Pattie. You can add an extra egg if necessary, although the tuna is usually wet enough that it isn't required.
7. Refrigerate for 30-60 minutes, or even overnight, after forming 6 patties. This will make them more manageable.
8. Remove from the refrigerator and coat in a panko crumb and parmesan cheese mixture.
9. Press your chosen zone - "Zone 1" or "Zone 2" and then rotate the knob to select "Air Fry".
10. Set the temperature to 200 degrees C, and then set the time for 5 minutes to preheat.
11. After preheating, spray the Air-Fryer basket of each zone with cooking spray, arrange them in a single layer, and spritz them with cooking spray.
12. Slide the basket into the Air Fryer and set the time for 4 minutes.
13. Carefully turn them and cook 4 minutes longer.
14. After cooking time is completed, place them on a serving plate and serve.

Serving Suggestions: Serve with lemon wedges.
Variation Tip: You can also add a teaspoon of sriracha.
Nutritional Information per Serving:
Calories: 387 | Fat: 17g | Sat Fat: 7g | Carbohydrates: 21g | Fibre: 2g | Sugar: 4g | Protein: 38g

Garlicky Teriyaki Salmon

Preparation Time: 10 minutes | Cooking Time: 15 minutes | Servings: 3

Ingredients:

- 8 tsp Less Sodium Teriyaki
- 3 tsp honey
- 2 cubes of frozen garlic
- 2 tsp extra virgin olive oil
- 3 pieces of wild salmon

Preparation:

1. Whisk everything together to make the marinade.
2. Pour over defrosted fish and marinate for 20 minutes.
3. Press your chosen zone - "Zone 1" or "Zone 2" and then rotate the knob to select "Air Fry".
4. Set the temperature to 175 degrees C, and then set the time for 5 minutes to preheat.
5. After preheating, place a foil sheet on each basket, spray the Air-Fryer basket of each zone with cooking spray, arrange them in a single layer, and spritz them with cooking spray.
6. Slide the basket into the Air Fryer and set the time for 12 minutes.
7. Carefully turn them and cook them 6 minutes longer.
8. After cooking time is completed, place them on a serving plate and serve.

Serving Suggestions: Serve with roasted veggies.
Variation Tip: You can also add a teaspoon of red pepper flakes.
Nutritional Information per Serving:
Calories: 198 | Fat: 9g | Sat Fat: 1g | Carbohydrates: 30g | Fibre: 0.1g | Sugar: 27g | Protein: 0.2g

Salmon Cakes with Mayonnaise

Preparation Time: 15 minutes | Cooking Time: 10 minutes | Servings: 4

Ingredients:

60g mayonnaise
1 tablespoon Sriracha

Salmon Cakes:
455g skinless salmon fillets, cut into 2.5cm pieces
30g almond flour
1 egg, lightly beaten
1½ teaspoon seafood seasoning
1 green onion, coarsely chopped
Cooking spray

Preparation:

1. In a small mixing dish, combine mayonnaise and Sriracha.
2. To the Sriracha mayo, add the salmon, almond flour, egg, 1½ teaspoons seafood spice, and green onion; pulse quickly for 4 to 5 seconds until ingredients are combined, but small chunks of salmon remain.
3. Spray hands with cooking spray and line a platter with waxed paper. Transfer the salmon mixture to a plate in 8 tiny patties. Refrigerate for about 15 minutes or until cool and stiff.
4. Press your chosen zone - "Zone 1" or "Zone 2" and then rotate the knob to select "Air Fry".
5. Set the temperature to 200 degrees C, and then set the time for 5 minutes to preheat.
6. After preheating, spray the Air-Fryer basket of each zone with cooking spray, arrange them in a single layer, and spritz them with cooking spray.
7. Slide the basket into the Air Fryer and set the time for 6 minutes.
8. Carefully turn them and cook them 2 minutes longer.
9. After cooking time is completed, place them on a serving plate and serve.

Serving Suggestions: Garnish with sesame seeds.
Variation Tip: You can also use coconut flour.
Nutritional Information per Serving:
Calories: 340 | Fat: 24g | Sat Fat: 4g | Carbohydrates: 3g | Fibre: 1g | Sugar: 0.7g | Protein: 25g

Korean-Style Prawn Skewers

Preparation Time: 5 minutes | Cooking Time: 5 minutes | Servings: 5

Ingredients:

1 tablespoon olive oil
2 tablespoons tamari soy sauce
2 tablespoons honey
2 tablespoons Korean Gochujang
1 tablespoon lemon juice
1 teaspoon minced garlic
900g peeled and cleaned prawns

Preparation:

1. Before usage, soak bamboo skewers in water for 30 minutes.
2. Combine olive oil, soy sauce, honey, Korean Gochujang, lemon juice, and garlic in a mixing bowl.
3. Toss the prawns into the bowl and toss to coat.
4. Marinate for about 30 minutes. Thread about 5 prawns to each skewer.
5. Press your chosen zone - "Zone 1" or "Zone 2" and then rotate the knob to select "Air Fry".
6. Set the temperature to 175 degrees C, and then set the time for 5 minutes to preheat.
7. After preheating, spray the Air-Fryer basket of each zone with cooking spray, arrange them in a single layer, and spritz them with cooking spray.
8. Slide the basket into the Air Fryer and set the time for 3 minutes.
9. Carefully turn them and cook them 2 minutes longer.
10. After cooking time is completed, place them on a serving plate and serve.

Serving Suggestions: Garnish with sesame seeds.
Variation Tip: You can use regular soy sauce.
Nutritional Information per Serving:
Calories: 76 | Fat: 2g | Sat Fat: 1g | Carbohydrates: 3g | Fibre: 1g | Sugar: 2g | Protein: 12g

Sweet Fried Salmon

Preparation Time: 10 minutes | Cooking Time: 10 minutes | Servings: 2

Ingredients:

- 2 salmon fillets
- 2 tablespoons butter
- 1 tablespoon brown sugar
- ½ teaspoon parsley
- ½ teaspoon garlic powder
- ½ teaspoon salt
- ¼ teaspoon pepper

Preparation:

1. Add brown sugar, garlic powder, parsley, salt and pepper in a bowl. Mix well.
2. Place salmon fillets in the mixture and rub generously with it.
3. Meanwhile, Grease basket of Ninja Foodi 2-Basket Air Fryer.
4. Press your chosen zone - "Zone 1" or "Zone 2" and then rotate the knob to select "Air Fry".
5. Set the temperature to 180 degrees C and then set the time for 5 minutes to preheat.
6. After preheating, arrange salmon fillets into the zone 1 and zone 2 of the basket and top them with butter.
7. Slide the basket into the Air Fryer and set the time for 10 minutes.
8. After cooking time is completed, remove the salmon fillets from Air Fryer and serve hot.

Serving Suggestions: Serve with chopped mint leaves on the top.

Variation Tip: Use skinless salmon fillets.

Nutritional Information per Serving:

Calories: 333 | Fat: 17g | Sat Fat: 6.2g | Carbohydrates: 16.7g | Fibre: 0.1g | Sugar: 16.1g | Protein: 29.5g

Air Fried Salmon Fillets

Preparation Time: 5 minutes | Cooking Time: 10 minutes | Servings: 2

Ingredients:

- 2 skin-on salmon fillets
- 2 garlic cloves, minced
- 1 teaspoon fresh Italian parsley
- 2 tablespoons butter, melted
- Salt and pepper, to taste

Preparation:

1. Grease basket of Ninja Foodi 2-Basket Air Fryer.
2. Press your chosen zone - "Zone 1" or "Zone 2" and then rotate the knob to select "Air Fry".
3. Set the temperature to 180 degrees C and then set the time for 5 minutes to preheat.
4. Take a bowl, add melted butter, parsley and garlic. Mix together.
5. Season fresh salmon fillets with salt and black pepper.
6. Place the salmon fillets in the butter mixture
7. After preheating, arrange salmon fillets into the basket of each zone.
8. Slide the basket into the Air Fryer and set the time for 10 minutes.
9. After cooking time is completed, remove the salmon fillets from Air Fryer and serve hot.

Serving Suggestions: Serve with the garnishing of spring onion.

Variation Tip: Use skinless salmon fillets.

Nutritional Information per Serving:

Calories: 107 | Fat: 26.5g | Sat Fat: 10.3g | Carbohydrates: 1g | Fibre: 0.1g | Sugar: 0.1g | Protein: 28.3g

Delicious Cod Cakes

Preparation Time: 10 minutes | **Cooking Time:** 10 minutes | **Servings:** 2

▶ Ingredients:

- 150g cod fillets
- 55g panko breadcrumbs
- 1 small egg
- 1 tablespoon mayonnaise
- 1 tablespoon sweet chili sauce
- 1 tablespoon fresh chopped coriander
- ⅛ teaspoon salt
- ⅛ teaspoon ground black pepper

▶ Preparation:

1. Grease basket of Ninja Foodi 2-Basket Air Fryer.
2. Press your chosen zone - "Zone 1" or "Zone 2" and then rotate the knob to select "Air Fry".
3. Set the heat to 200 degrees C and then set the time for 5 minutes to preheat.
4. Take a food processor, add cod fillets and process until crumbly.
5. Take a bowl, add crumbled fish, breadcrumbs, chili sauce, mayo, egg, salt, coriander and pepper. Stir until well combined.
6. Shape the mixture into patties.
7. After preheating, arrange patties into the basket of each zone.
8. Slide the basket into the Air Fryer and set the time for 10 minutes.
9. After cooking time is completed, remove the patties from Air Fryer and serve hot.

Serving Suggestions: Serve with lime wedges.

Variation Tip: Chop the fish finely instead of using a food processor.

Nutritional Information per Serving:
Calories: 236 | Fat: 6.9g | Sat Fat: 1.7g | Carbohydrates: 9.1g | Fibre: 0.1g | Sugar: 3.7g | Protein: 18.3g

Lemony Salmon

Preparation Time: 10 minutes | **Cooking Time:** 10 minutes | **Servings:** 4

▶ Ingredients:

- 2 lemons, zested and sliced
- ½ teaspoon salt
- 4 (110g) salmon fillets
- 1 tablespoon avocado oil
- 1 teaspoon fresh black pepper
- 1 teaspoon garlic powder

▶ Preparation:

1. Grease basket of Ninja Foodi 2-Basket Air Fryer.
2. Press your chosen zone - "Zone 1" or "Zone 2" and then rotate the knob to select "Air Fry".
3. Set the heat to 190 degrees C and then set the time for 5 minutes to preheat.
4. Season the salmon fillets with lemon, salt, garlic powder, black pepper and avocado oil.
5. After preheating, arrange 2 salmon fillets into the basket of each zone.
6. Slide the basket into the Air Fryer and set the time for 10 minutes.
7. After cooking time is completed, remove the salmon fillets from Air Fryer and serve hot.

Serving Suggestions: Serve with chopped parsley on the top.

Variation Tip: Use skin-on salmon fillets.

Nutritional Information per Serving:
Calories: 167 | Fat: 7.6g | Sat Fat: 1.1g | Carbohydrates: 3.8g | Fibre: 1.2g | Sugar: 0.9g | Protein: 22.5g

Sweet and Spicy Salmon

Preparation Time: 10 minutes | Cooking Time: 12 minutes | Servings: 2

Ingredients:

- 2 salmon fillets
- ¾ teaspoon toasted sesame oil
- 1 teaspoon sesame seeds
- ½ tablespoon low-sodium soy sauce
- ½ tablespoon honey
- ¼ teaspoon crushed chili flakes
- Salt and pepper, to taste

Preparation:

1. In a shallow dish, add soy sauce, salt, pepper and oil. Whisk well.
2. Pour the mixture over salmon-fillets and rub all over the fish.
3. Cover the dish and place the mixture in refrigerator for about 15 minutes.
4. Remove the salmon fillets from refrigerator and shake off the excess marinade.
5. Line each basket of "Zone 1" and "Zone 2" of Ninja Foodi 2-Basket Air Fryer with a piece of foil.
6. Press your chosen zone - "Zone 1" or "Zone 2" and then rotate the knob to select "Air Fry".
7. Set the heat to 180 degrees C and then set the time for 5 minutes to preheat.
8. After preheating, arrange salmon fillets into the basket of each zone.
9. Brush with honey and sprinkle with chili flakes and sesame seeds.
10. Slide the basket into the Air Fryer and set the time for 12 minutes.
11. After cooking time is completed, remove the salmon fillets from Air Fryer and serve hot.

Serving Suggestions: Serve with lemon wedges.
Variation Tip: Use maple syrup for sweet taste.
Nutritional Information per Serving:
Calories: 335 | Fat: 16.6g | Sat Fat: 2.8g | Carbohydrates: 18.3g | Fibre: 1g | Sugar: 14.1g | Protein: 29.8g

Air Fryer Salmon with Asparagus

Preparation Time: 10 minutes | Cooking Time: 13 minutes | Servings: 4

Ingredients:

- 3 tablespoons lemon juice
- 4 tablespoons fresh dill, roughly chopped
- 4 salmon fillets
- 2 tablespoons olive oil
- 4 tablespoons fresh parsley, roughly chopped
- 900g asparagus
- Salt and pepper, to taste

Preparation:

1. In a small dish, mix lemon juice, olive oil, salt, pepper, dill and parsley.
2. Add salmon fillets in the mixture, coat well and set aside.
3. Now, add asparagus in the dill mixture and mix well.
4. Grease basket of Ninja Foodi 2-Basket Air Fryer.
5. Press your chosen zone - "Zone 1" or "Zone 2" and then rotate the knob to select "Air Fry".
6. Set the heat to 200 degrees C and then set the time for 5 minutes to preheat.
7. After preheating, arrange asparagus into the basket of each zone.
8. Slide the basket into the Air Fryer and set the time for 13 minutes.
9. After 3 minutes of cooking, arrange 2 salmon fillets on top of asparagus in each basket.
10. After cooking time is completed, remove the salmon fillets and asparagus from Air Fryer and serve hot.

Serving Suggestions: Serve with lemon wedges on the top.
Variation Tip: Don't use skinless salmon fillets.
Nutritional Information per Serving:
Calories: 296 | Fat: 14.3g | Sat Fat: 2g | Carbohydrates: 6.1g | Fibre: 0.3g | Sugar: 5.7g | Protein: 37g

Lemon Garlic Tilapia

Preparation Time: 10 minutes | **Cooking Time:** 12 minutes | **Servings:** 4

Ingredients:

- 4 tilapia fillets
- 1 teaspoon lemon pepper seasoning
- 1 teaspoon garlic powder
- 1 teaspoon onion powder
- Salt and black pepper, to taste

Preparation:

1. In a shallow dish, add lemon pepper seasoning, garlic powder, onion powder, salt and black pepper. Mix well.
2. Coat the tilapia fillets with oil and then rub with spice mixture.
3. Grease basket of Ninja Foodi 2-Basket Air Fryer.
4. Press your chosen zone - "Zone 1" or "Zone 2" and then rotate the knob to select "Air Fry".
5. Set the temperature to 180 degrees C and then set the time for 5 minutes to preheat.
6. After preheating, arrange tilapia fillets into the basket of each zone.
7. Slide the basket into the Air Fryer and set the time for 12 minutes.
8. While cooking, flip the tilapia fillets once halfway through.
9. After cooking time is completed, remove the tilapia fillets and from Air Fryer and serve hot.

Serving Suggestions: Serve with lemon wedges on the top.
Variation Tip: Black pepper can be replaced with cayenne pepper.
Nutritional Information per Serving:
Calories: 99 | Fat: 1.1g | Sat Fat: 0.5g | Carbohydrates: 1.3g | Fibre: 0.2g | Sugar: 0.4g | Protein: 21.3g

Tasty Breaded Tilapia

Preparation Time: 10 minutes | **Cooking Time:** 12 minutes | **Servings:** 6

Ingredients:

- 4 large eggs
- ½ teaspoon cayenne pepper powder
- 4 large tilapia fillets, patted dry
- 6 tablespoons plain flour
- 300g breadcrumbs
- Salt and pepper, to taste

Preparation:

1. In a shallow dish, beat eggs and add cayenne pepper, plain flour, salt and pepper in it. Mix well.
2. Add breadcrumbs in another bowl and set aside.
3. Dip the tilapia fillets into egg mixture and then coat with the breadcrumbs mixture.
4. Grease basket of Ninja Foodi 2-Basket Air Fryer.
5. Press your chosen zone - "Zone 1" or "Zone 2" and then rotate the knob to select "Air Fry".
6. Set the heat to 180 degrees C and then set the time for 5 minutes to preheat.
7. After preheating, arrange tilapia fillets into the basket of each zone.
8. Slide the basket into the Air Fryer and set the time for 12 minutes.
9. While cooking, flip the tilapia fillets once halfway through.
10. After cooking time is completed, remove the tilapia fillets and from Air Fryer and serve hot.

Serving Suggestions: Serve with hot sauce.
Variation Tip: You can use oregano to enhance taste.
Nutritional Information per Serving:
Calories: 352 | Fat: 6.9g | Sat Fat: 2g | Carbohydrates: 45.3g | Fibre: 2.7g | Sugar: 3.6g | Protein: 26.2g

Spicy Cajun Cod Fillets

Preparation Time: 15 minutes | Cooking Time: 16 minutes | Servings: 6

Ingredients:

- 6 cod fillets
- 3 tablespoons almond flour
- 1 teaspoon smoked paprika
- 30g gluten-free flour
- 2 teaspoons Cajun seasoning
- ½ teaspoon garlic powder
- Salt and pepper, to taste

Preparation:

1. Add almond flour, smoked paprika, gluten-free flour, Cajun seasoning, garlic powder, salt and pepper in a shallow dish. Whisk well.
2. Coat the fillets with flour mixture and refrigerate for about 2 hours.
3. Grease basket of Ninja Foodi 2-Basket Air Fryer.
4. Press your chosen zone - "Zone 1" or "Zone 2" and then rotate the knob to select "Air Fry".
5. Set the temperature to 200 degrees C and then set the time for 5 minutes to preheat.
6. After preheating, arrange the cod fillets into the basket of each zone.
7. Slide the basket into the Air Fryer and set the time for 16 minutes.
8. While cooking, flip the cod fillets once halfway through.
9. After cooking time is completed, remove the cod fillets from Air Fryer and serve hot.

Serving Suggestions: Serve with hot sauce.
Variation Tip: Regular flour can be used instead of gluten-free flour.
Nutritional Information per Serving:
Calories: 139 | Fat: 1.1g | Sat Fat: 0.2g | Carbohydrates: 4.4g | Fibre: 0.7g | Sugar: 0.2g | Protein: 26.3g

Crispy and Spicy Catfish

Preparation Time: 10 minutes | Cooking Time: 20 minutes | Servings: 2

Ingredients:

- 455g catfish filets
- 3 drops hot sauce
- 2½ tablespoons plain flour
- ¼ teaspoon black pepper
- 120ml buttermilk
- 80g polenta
- 1 tablespoon Cajun seasoning
- Salt, to taste

Preparation:

1. In a shallow dish, add hot sauce, plain flour, black pepper, buttermilk, polenta, Cajun seasoning and salt. Mix well.
2. Add the catfish fillets and coat evenly with the mixture.
3. Grease basket of Ninja Foodi 2-Basket Air Fryer.
4. Press your chosen zone - "Zone 1" or "Zone 2" and then rotate the knob to select "Air Fry".
5. Set the temperature to 200 degrees C and then set the time for 5 minutes to preheat.
6. After preheating, arrange catfish fillets into the basket of each zone.
7. Slide the basket into the Air Fryer and set the time for 20 minutes.
8. While cooking, flip the fish fillets once halfway through.
9. After cooking time is completed, remove the fish fillets from Air Fryer and serve hot.

Serving Suggestions: Serve with garlic mayo dip.
Variation Tip: Use the seasoning of your choice.
Nutritional Information per Serving:
Calories: 784 | Fat: 36.5g | Sat Fat: 6g | Carbohydrates: 68.1g | Fibre: 7g | Sugar: 8.1g | Protein: 48.8g

Garlic Butter Prawns with Parsley

Preparation Time: 15 minutes | Cooking Time: 8 minutes | Servings: 6

Ingredients:

- 900g fresh prawns
- 175g unsalted butter, melted
- 6 tablespoons fresh parsley, chopped
- 4 tablespoons olive oil
- 4 teaspoons minced garlic
- Salt and pepper, to taste

Preparation:

1. Add butter, parsley, olive oil, minced garlic, salt and pepper in a large bowl. Whisk well.
2. Add in prawns in the mixture and toss to coat well.
3. Press "Zone 1" and "Zone 2" of Ninja Foodi 2-Basket Air Fryer and then rotate the knob for each zone to select "Bake".
4. Set the temperature to 230 degrees C and then set the time for 5 minutes to preheat.
5. After preheating, arrange 1 pan into the basket of each zone.
6. Slide the basket into the Air Fryer and set the time for 8 minutes.
7. After cooking time is completed, remove the pans from Air Fryer and serve hot.

Serving Suggestions: Serve with the garnishing of fresh herbs.

Variation Tip: Frozen prawns can also be used.

Nutritional Information per Serving:

Calories: 350 | Fat: 26.2g | Sat Fat: 12.5g | Carbohydrates: 2.4g | Fibre: 0.1g | Sugar: 0g | Protein: 26.2g

Simple Fried Salmon

Preparation Time: 10 minutes | Cooking Time: 10 minutes | Servings: 4

Ingredients:

- 4 (150g) salmon fillets
- Salt and ground black pepper, as required
- 2 tablespoons olive oil

Preparation:

1. Grease basket of Ninja Foodi 2-Basket Air Fryer.
2. Press your chosen zone - "Zone 1" or "Zone 2" and then rotate the knob to select "Air Fry".
3. Set the temperature to 180 degrees C and then set the time for 5 minutes to preheat.
4. Season each salmon fillet with salt and black pepper and then coat with the oil.
5. After preheating, arrange salmon fillets in the basket of each zone.
6. Slide the basket into the Air Fryer and set the time for 10 minutes.
7. After cooking time is completed, remove the salmon fillets from Air Fryer and serve hot.

Serving Suggestions: Serve with the garnishing of spring onion.

Variation Tip: Use skinless salmon fillets.

Nutritional Information per Serving:

Calories: 285 | Fat: 17.5g | Sat Fat: 2.5g | Carbohydrates: 0g | Fibre: 0g | Sugar: 0g | Protein: 33g

Spicy Salmon with Lemon

Preparation Time: 10 minutes | Cooking Time: 8 minutes | Servings: 4

Ingredients:

- 4 (150g) salmon fillets
- ½ teaspoon red chili powder
- Salt and ground black pepper, as required
- 1 lemon, cut into slices

Preparation:

1. Grease basket of Ninja Foodi 2-Basket Air Fryer.
2. Press your chosen zone - "Zone 1" or "Zone 2" and then rotate the knob to select "Air Fry".
3. Set the temperature to 190 degrees C and then set the time for 5 minutes to preheat.
4. Season the salmon fillets with chili powder, salt, and black pepper evenly.
5. After preheating, arrange salmon fillets in the basket of each zone.
6. Arrange lemon slices over each salmon fillet.
7. Slide the basket into the Air Fryer and set the time for 8 minutes.
8. After cooking time is completed, remove the salmon fillets from Air Fryer and serve hot.

Serving Suggestions: Serve alongside the steamed green beans.

Variation Tip: Be sure that salmon should look bright and shiny before buying.

Nutritional Information per Serving:
Calories: 16 | Fat: 0g | Sat Fat: 0g | Carbohydrates: 2.1g | Fibre: 0.1g | Sugar: 0.7g | Protein: 0.2g

Spicy Fried Scallops

Preparation Time: 4 minutes | Cooking Time: 6 minutes | Servings: 2

Ingredients:

- 455g scallops
- 1 teaspoon paprika
- 2 tablespoons softened butter
- 2 teaspoons salt-free lemon pepper seasoning
- Salt and black pepper, to taste

Preparation:

1. In a large dish, place the scallops, butter, paprika, lemon pepper seasoning, salt, and black pepper and toss to coat well.
2. Grease basket of Ninja Foodi 2-Basket Air Fryer.
3. Press your chosen zone - "Zone 1" or "Zone 2" and then rotate the knob to select "Bake".
4. Set the temperature to 200 degrees C and then set the time for 5 minutes to preheat.
5. After preheating, arrange the scallops into the basket of each zone.
6. Slide the basket into the Air Fryer and set the time for 6 minutes.
7. After cooking time is completed, remove the scallops from Air Fryer and serve hot.

Serving Suggestions: Serve with the drizzling of extra melted butter.

Variation Tip: Make sure to pat-dry the scallops before using.

Nutritional Information per Serving:
Calories: 305 | Fat: 13.4g | Sat Fat: 7.5g | Carbohydrates: 6g | Fibre: 0.4g | Sugar: 0.1g | Protein: 38.3g

Sweet & Sour Salmon

Preparation Time: 10 minutes | **Cooking Time:** 12 minutes | **Servings:** 4

Ingredients:

- 180ml soy sauce
- 180g maple syrup
- 6 teaspoons fresh lemon juice
- 2 teaspoons water
- 8 (90g) salmon fillets

Preparation:

1. In a small bowl, mix together the soy sauce, maple syrup, lemon juice and water.
2. Reserve about half of the mixture in another small bowl.
3. Add salmon fillets in the remaining mixture and coat well.
4. Cover the bowl and refrigerate to marinate for about 2 hours.
5. Remove the salmon fillets from refrigerator and shake off the excess marinade.
6. Line each basket of "Zone 1" and "Zone 2" of Ninja Foodi 2-Basket Air Fryer with a piece of foil.
7. Press your chosen zone - "Zone 1" or "Zone 2" and then rotate the knob to select "Air Fry".
8. Set the temperature to 180 degrees C and then set the time for 5 minutes to preheat.
9. After preheating, arrange salmon fillets in the basket of each zone.
10. Slide the basket into the Air Fryer and set the time for 12 minutes.
11. After cooking time is completed, remove the salmon fillets from Air Fryer. Serve hot.

Serving Suggestions: Garnish with sesame seeds.
Variation Tip: Use freshly squeezed lemon juice.
Nutritional Information per Serving:
Calories: 335 | Fat: 16.6g | Sat Fat: 2.8g | Carbohydrates: 18.3g | Fibre: 1g | Sugar: 14.1g | Protein: 29.8g

Herbed Salmon with Asparagus

Preparation Time: 15 minutes | **Cooking Time:** 11 minutes | **Servings:** 4

Ingredients:

- 4 (150g) boneless salmon fillets
- 3 tablespoons fresh lemon juice
- 2 tablespoons olive oil
- 4 tablespoons fresh parsley, roughly chopped
- 4 tablespoons fresh dill, roughly chopped
- 400g asparagus
- Salt and ground black pepper, as required

Preparation:

1. In a small bowl, mix together the lemon juice, oil, herbs, salt, and black pepper.
2. In a large bowl, mix together the salmon and ¾ of oil mixture.
3. In a second large bowl, add the asparagus and remaining oil mixture and mix well.
4. Grease basket of Ninja Foodi 2-Basket Air Fryer.
5. Press your chosen zone - "Zone 1" or "Zone 2" and then rotate the knob to select "Air Fry".
6. Set the temperature to 200 degrees C and then set the time for 5 minutes to preheat.
7. After preheating, arrange asparagus into the basket of each zone.
8. Slide the basket into the Air Fryer and set the time for 11 minutes.
9. After 3 minutes of cooking, arrange salmon fillets on top of asparagus in each basket.
10. After cooking time is completed, remove the salmon fillets and asparagus from Air Fryer and serve hot.

Serving Suggestions: Serve alongside the lemon slices.
Variation Tip: Don't use frozen salmon fillets.
Nutritional Information per Serving:
Calories: 320 | Fat: 17.9g | Sat Fat: 2.7g | Carbohydrates: 6.6g | Fibre: 3g | Sugar: 2.4g | Protein: 36.3g

Chapter 5 Poultry Mains Recipes

Chicken & Rice Stuffed Peppers

Preparation Time: 15 minutes | Cooking Time: 15 minutes | Servings: 4

Ingredients:

- 230g prepared pesto
- 50g shredded Havarti cheese
- 280g shredded rotisserie chicken
- 390g cooked brown rice
- 4 medium yellow peppers

Preparation:

1. Cut peppers in half, remove stems and seeds.
2. In a bowl, combine chicken, rice and pesto.
3. Fill the peppers with chicken mixture.
4. Grease basket of Ninja Foodi 2-Basket Air Fryer.
5. Press your chosen zone - "Zone 1" or "Zone 2" and then rotate the knob to select "Air Fry".
6. Set temperature to 200 degrees C and then set the time for 5 minutes to preheat.
7. After preheating, arrange peppers into the basket of each zone.
8. Slide the basket into the Air Fryer and set the time for 10minutes.
9. After 10minutes, sprinkle cheese on top and set the temperature to 175 degrees C.
10. Set the time for 5 minutes.
11. After cooking time is completed, remove it from Air Fryer and serve hot.

Serving Suggestions: Serve with fresh salad.
Variation Tip: You can use fresh herbs of your choice.
Nutritional Information per Serving:
Calories: 520 | Fat: 7.8g | Sat Fat: 2g | Carbohydrates: 86g | Fibre: 4.9g | Sugar: 0g | Protein: 27.4g

Spiced Duck Legs

Preparation Time: 10 minutes | Cooking Time: 30 minutes | Servings: 2

Ingredients:

- 2 duck legs
- 2 tablespoons fresh parsley, chopped
- 2 teaspoons five-spice powder
- 2 garlic cloves, minced
- Salt and ground black pepper, as required

Preparation:

1. In a bowl, add the garlic, parsley, five-spice powder, salt and black pepper and mix until well combined.
2. Rub the duck legs with garlic mixture generously.
3. Grease basket of Ninja Foodi 2-Basket Air Fryer.
4. Press your chosen zone - "Zone 1" or "Zone 2" and then rotate the knob to select "Air Fry".
5. Set the temperature to 170 degrees C and then set the time for 5 minutes to preheat.
6. After preheating, arrange the duck legs into the basket of each zone.
7. Slide the basket into the Air Fryer and set the time for 30 minutes.
8. After cooking time is completed, remove the duck legs from Air Fryer and serve hot.

Serving Suggestions: Serve alongside the fresh salad.
Variation Tip: Make sure that the skin of duck legs is clear and soft.
Nutritional Information per Serving:
Calories: 188 | Fat: 4.5g | Sat Fat: 1g | Carbohydrates: 4.3g | Fibre: 6.6g | Sugar: 0.1g | Protein: 25.5g

Beer-Braised Duck Breast

Preparation Time: 10 minutes | **Cooking Time:** 15 minutes | **Servings:** 2

► **Ingredients:**

1 duck breast
1 teaspoon mustard
1 tablespoon fresh thyme, chopped
240ml beer
1 tablespoon olive oil
Salt and ground black pepper, as required

► **Preparation:**

1. In a bowl, place the beer, oil, mustard, thyme, salt, and black pepper and mix well.
2. Add the duck breasts and coat with marinade generously.
3. Cover and refrigerate for about 4 hours.
4. Remove from the refrigerator and with a piece of foil, cover each duck breast.
5. Press "Zone 1" of Ninja Foodi 2-Basket Air Fryer and then rotate the knob for each zone to select "Air Fry".
6. Set the temperature to 200 degrees C and then set the time for 5 minutes to preheat.
7. After preheating, arrange the duck breast into the basket of each zone.
8. Slide the basket into the Air Fryer and set the time for 15 minutes.
9. After 5 minutes of cooking, remove the foil from duck breast and set the temperature to 180 degrees C.
10. After cooking time is completed, remove the duck breast from Air Fryer.
11. Place the duck breasts onto a cutting board for about 5 minutes before slicing.
12. With a sharp knife, cut each duck breast into desired size slices and serve.

Serving Suggestions: Serve alongside the cranberry sauce.
Variation Tip: You can use oil of your choice.
Nutritional Information per Serving:
Calories: 226 | Fat: 10.8g | Sat Fat: 1.1g | Carbohydrates: 5.7g | Fibre: 0.7g | Sugar: 0.1g | Protein: 18.7g

Herbed Lime Gingered Turkey Legs

Preparation Time: 10 minutes | **Cooking Time:** 30 minutes | **Servings:** 2

► **Ingredients:**

2 turkey legs
2 tablespoons olive oil
1 tablespoon fresh lime juice
2 garlic cloves, minced
1 tablespoon fresh
rosemary, minced
1 teaspoon fresh lime zest, finely grated
Salt and ground black pepper, as required

► **Preparation:**

1. In a large baking dish, mix together the garlic, rosemary, lime zest, oil, lime juice, salt, and black pepper.
2. Add the turkey legs and generously coat with marinade.
3. Refrigerate to marinate for about 6-8 hours.
4. Grease basket of Ninja Foodi 2-Basket Air Fryer.
5. Press your chosen zone - "Zone 1" or "Zone 2" and then rotate the knob to select "Air Fry".
6. Set the temperature to 175 degrees C and then set the time for 5 minutes to preheat.
7. After preheating, arrange the turkey legs into the basket of each zone.
8. Slide the basket into the Air Fryer and set the time for 30 minutes.
9. While cooking, flip the turkey legs once halfway through.
10. After cooking time is completed, remove the turkey legs from Air Fryer and serve hot.

Serving Suggestions: Serve with buttery mashed potatoes.
Variation Tip: Try to use fresh turkey legs.
Nutritional Information per Serving:
Calories: 284 | Fat: 21.3g | Sat Fat: 4.3g | Carbohydrates: 4.1g | Fibre: 1g | Sugar: 0.4g | Protein: 20.2g

Homemade Chicken Tenders

Preparation Time: 5 minutes | Cooking Time: 10 minutes | Servings: 2

Ingredients:

225g chicken breasts
30g flour
1 egg
⅛ teaspoon paprika
¼ teaspoon onion powder
¼ teaspoon garlic powder
¼ teaspoon Italian seasoning
25g panko breadcrumbs
Salt and pepper, to taste

Preparation:

1. Cut chicken breasts into thin 2.5 cm strips.
2. Set up the batter by putting flour and eggs in two separate bowls. Whisk the eggs.
3. In a large bowl, mix together panko breadcrumbs, garlic powder, onion powder, paprika, Italian seasoning and salt and pepper.
4. Dip chicken breasts into flour, then the eggs, and then finally breadcrumbs.
5. Grease basket of Ninja Foodi 2-Basket Air Fryer.
6. Press your chosen zone - "Zone 1" or "Zone 2" and then rotate the knob to select "Air Fry".
7. Set temperature to 200 degrees C and then set the time for 5 minutes to preheat.
8. After preheating, arrange coated chicken into the basket of each zone.
9. Slide the basket into the Air Fryer and set the time for 7-10 minutes.
10. After cooking time is completed, remove from Air Fryer.
11. Cut each portion into half and serve hot.

Serving Suggestions: Serve with your favourite fresh salad.
Variation Tip: You can add fresh herbs.
Nutritional Information per Serving:
Calories: 308 | Fat: 10.9g | Sat Fat: 3g | Carbohydrates: 12.8g | Fibre: 0.5g | Sugar: 0.5g | Protein: 37.3

Breaded Chicken Cutlets

Preparation Time: 8 minutes | Cooking Time: 10 minutes | Servings: 2

Ingredients:

2 chicken cutlets
25g Italian breadcrumbs
1 egg
¼ teaspoon paprika
⅛ teaspoon garlic powder
⅛ teaspoon onion powder
Salt and pepper, to taste

Preparation:

1. Rub the chicken with salt and pepper.
2. In a bowl, whisk the eggs.
3. Take another bowl and combine the breadcrumbs and seasoning.
4. Dip chicken cutlet in the eggs and then lay it in breadcrumbs. Do this on the either sides of the chicken cutlet.
5. Grease basket of Ninja Foodi 2-Basket Air Fryer.
6. Press your chosen zone - "Zone 1" or "Zone 2" and then rotate the knob to select "Air Fry".
7. Set temperature to 200 degrees C and then set the time for 5 minutes to preheat.
8. After preheating, arrange 1 chicken cutlet into the basket of each zone.
9. Slide the basket into the Air Fryer and set the time for 10 to 12 minutes.
10. After cooking time is completed, remove the chicken cutlets from Air Fryer and place each onto a platter for about 10 minutes before serving.
11. Serve and enjoy.

Serving Suggestions: Serve with steamed veggies.
Variation Tip: Fresh chicken should have a pinkish colour.
Nutritional Information per Serving:
Calories: 353 | Fat: 13.3g | Sat Fat: 3.7g | Carbohydrates: 10.3g | Fibre: 0.8g | Sugar: 1.1g | Protein: 45.2g

Spiced Chicken Wings

Preparation Time: 10 minutes | Cooking Time: 35 minutes | Servings: 3

Ingredients:

- 455g whole chicken wings
- 1 teaspoon garlic powder
- ½ teaspoon garlic salt
- ¼ teaspoon cayenne pepper
- ¼ teaspoon baking soda
- ¼ teaspoon ground allspice
- ¼ teaspoon pepper
- ½ teaspoon mustard
- ½ teaspoon ginger
- ½ teaspoon nutmeg

Preparation:

1. In a large bowl, combine garlic powder, mustard, ginger, nutmeg, garlic salt, allspice, baking soda, pepper and cayenne pepper.
2. Cut chicken wings into sections.
3. Add to the bowl and stir firmly to coat.
4. Grease basket of Ninja Foodi 2-Basket Air Fryer.
5. Press your chosen zone - "Zone 1" or "Zone 2" and then rotate the knob to select "Air Fry".
6. Set the heat to 150 degrees C and then set the time for 5 minutes to preheat.
7. After preheating, arrange chicken wings into the basket of each zone.
8. Slide the basket into the Air Fryer and set the time for 30 to 35 minutes.
9. After cooking time is completed, remove the chicken legs from Air Fryer and serve hot.

Serving Suggestions: Serve with roasted veggies.
Variation Tip: You can add fresh herbs of your choice.
Nutritional Information per Serving:
Calories: 91 | Fat: 6.4g | Sat Fat: 1.9g | Carbohydrates: 0.4g | Fibre: 0.1g | Sugar: 0.1g | Protein: 8.1g

Buttered Chicken Breast

Preparation Time: 2 minutes | Cooking Time: 10 minutes | Servings: 2

Ingredients:

- 2 boneless chicken breasts
- ⅛ teaspoon pepper
- 1 tablespoon butter
- ¼ teaspoon salt
- ⅛ teaspoon garlic powder

Preparation:

1. Melt butter and add in garlic powder, salt and pepper. Combine well.
2. Take a cutting board and place chicken breasts.
3. Coat chicken with butter mixture.
4. Grease basket of Ninja Foodi 2-Basket Air Fryer.
5. Press your chosen zone - "Zone 1" or "Zone 2" and then rotate the knob to select "Air Fry".
6. Set the heat to 195 degrees C and then set the time for 5 minutes to preheat.
7. After preheating, arrange chicken breasts into the basket of each zone.
8. Slide the basket into the Air Fryer and set the time for 10 to 15 minutes.
9. After cooking time is completed, remove the chicken breasts from Air Fryer and serve hot.

Serving Suggestions: Serve alongside the orange slices.
Variation Tip: You can adjust the amount of spices according to your taste.
Nutritional Information per Serving:
Calories: 318 | Fat: 16.1g | Sat Fat: 6.5g | Carbohydrates: 0.2g | Fibre: 0.1g | Sugar: 0g | Protein: 40.6g

Cheese Chicken Pockets

Preparation Time: 15 minutes | **Cooking Time:** 25 minutes | **Servings:** 4

Ingredients:

- 70g shredded rotisserie chicken
- 50g shredded cheddar cheese
- 4 tablespoons salsa
- 100g puff pastry sheets, refrigerated
- 1 tablespoon taco seasoning
- 60g sour cream

Preparation:

1. In a bowl, combine salsa, sour cream and taco seasoning.
2. Unroll crescent rolls dough and separate into rectangles.
3. Place chicken onto the left side of each rectangle and top it with salsa mixture.
4. Sprinkle cheese on top.
5. Fold the dough and pinch edges to seal properly.
6. Grease basket of Ninja Foodi 2-Basket Air Fryer.
7. Press your chosen zone - "Zone 1" or "Zone 2" and then rotate the knob to select "Air Fry".
8. Set the heat to 190 degrees C and then set the time for 5 minutes to preheat.
9. After preheating, place pockets into the basket of each zone.
10. Slide the basket into the Air Fryer and set the time for 13 to 15 minutes.
11. After cooking time is completed, remove it from Air Fryer and serve hot.

Serving Suggestions: Serve with your favourite vegetables.
Variation Tip: You can adjust the amount of spices according to your taste.
Nutritional Information per Serving:
Calories: 343 | Fat: 17.6g | Sat Fat: 6.6g | Carbohydrates: 27.2g | Fibre: 0.8g | Sugar: 2.2g | Protein: 19.6g

Delicious Chicken Pesto Stuffed Peppers

Preparation Time: 15 minutes | **Cooking Time:** 15 minutes | **Servings:** 2

Ingredients:

- 140g shredded rotisserie chicken
- 195g cooked brown rice
- 2 medium yellow peppers
- 115g prepared pesto
- 25g shredded Havarti cheese

Preparation:

1. Cut peppers in half, remove stems and seeds.
2. In a bowl, combine chicken, rice and pesto.
3. Fill the peppers with chicken mixture.
4. Grease basket of Ninja Foodi 2-Basket Air Fryer.
5. Press your chosen zone - "Zone 1" or "Zone 2" and then rotate the knob to select "Air Fry".
6. Set temperature to 200 degrees C and then set the time for 5 minutes to preheat.
7. After preheating, arrange peppers into the basket of each zone.
8. Slide the basket into the Air Fryer and set the time for 10minutes.
9. After 10minutes, sprinkle cheese on top and set the temperature to 175 degrees C.
10. Set the time for 5 minutes.

After cooking time is completed, remove it from Air Fryer and serve hot.

Serving Suggestions: Serve alongside the lemon wedges.
Variation Tip: You can use fresh herbs of your choice.
Nutritional Information per Serving:
Calories: 488 | Fat: 4.6g | Sat Fat: 1.3g | Carbohydrates: 85.7g | Fibre: 4.9g | Sugar: 0.1g | Protein: 27.4g

Fried Chicken with Cheese and Pasta Sauce

Preparation Time: 10 minutes | Cooking Time: 20 minutes | Servings: 2

Ingredients:

- 2 boneless skinless chicken breast halves
- 25g breadcrumbs
- 25g grated Parmesan cheese
- 1 egg
- ⅛ teaspoon pepper
- 110g shredded mozzarella cheese
- 120g pasta sauce

Preparation:

1. In a shallow bowl, beat egg.
2. Take another bowl, add breadcrumbs, Parmesan cheese and pepper.
3. Dip chicken breast in egg and then coat with breadcrumbs mixture.
4. Grease basket of Ninja Foodi 2-Basket Air Fryer.
5. Press your chosen zone - "Zone 1" or "Zone 2" and then rotate the knob to select "Air Fry".
6. Set the heat to 190 degrees C and then set the time for 5 minutes to preheat.
7. After preheating, arrange chicken breast halves into the basket of each zone.
8. Slide the basket into the Air Fryer and set the time for 10 to 12 minutes.
9. While cooking, flip the chicken once halfway through and top with sauce and cheese.
10. After cooking time is completed, remove the chicken thighs from Air Fryer and serve hot.

Serving Suggestions: Serve with your favourite fresh salad.

Variation Tip: You can also add pasta sauce.

Nutritional Information per Serving:
Calories: 437 | Fat: 17g | Sat Fat: 5.4g | Carbohydrates: 19g | Fibre: 2.3g | Sugar: 6.5g | Protein: 49.3g

Air Fried Curry Chicken Drumsticks

Preparation Time: 30 minutes | Cooking Time: 15 minutes | Servings: 2

Ingredients:

- 225g chicken drumsticks
- 1 tablespoon olive oil
- ½ teaspoon salt, divided
- ¼ teaspoon garlic powder
- ¼ teaspoon onion salt
- 1 teaspoon curry powder

Preparation:

1. In a large bowl, place chicken and add salt and enough water to cover.
2. Let it sit for 15 minutes at room temperature.
3. Drain and pat dry.
4. In another bowl, mix together oil, curry powder, garlic powder, onion salt and remaining salt.
5. Add chicken into the mixture and toss to coat well.
6. Grease basket of Ninja Foodi 2-Basket Air Fryer.
7. Press your chosen zone - "Zone 1" or "Zone 2" and then rotate the knob to select "Air Fry".
8. Set the heat to 190 degrees C and then set the time for 5 minutes to preheat.
9. After preheating, arrange drumsticks into the basket of each zone.
10. Slide the basket into the Air Fryer and set the time for 15 to 17 minutes.
11. While cooking, flip the drumsticks once halfway through.
12. After cooking time is completed, remove the drumsticks from Air Fryer and serve hot.

Serving Suggestions: Serve with tomato ketchup or hot mix sauce.

Variation Tip: Coat the chicken with coating evenly.

Nutritional Information per Serving:
Calories: 256 | Fat: 13.6g | Sat Fat: 2.7g | Carbohydrates: 0.8g | Fibre: 0.4g | Sugar: 0.1g | Protein: 31.4g

Cheese Onion & Green Peppers Stuffed Chicken

Preparation Time: 10 minutes | **Cooking Time:** 15 minutes | **Servings:** 2

Ingredients:

- 2 boneless skinless chicken breast halves
- ½ onion, thinly sliced
- ½ teaspoon ground cumin
- ½ teaspoon chili powder
- ½ tablespoon olive oil
- ¼ medium green pepper, thinly sliced
- ¼ teaspoon salt
- ⅛ teaspoon garlic powder
- 50g cheddar cheese, cut into slices

Preparation:

1. Cut each chicken breast in the thickest part and fill with green peppers and onion.
2. In a small bowl, combine olive oil and seasonings.
3. Rub over chicken. Add cheese on the chicken breasts.
4. Grease basket of Ninja Foodi 2-Basket Air Fryer.
5. Press your chosen zone - "Zone 1" or "Zone 2" and then rotate the knob to select "Air Fry".
6. Set the heat to 190 degrees C and then set the time for 5 minutes to preheat.
7. After preheating, arrange chicken breasts into the basket of each zone.
8. Slide the basket into the Air Fryer and set the time for 15 minutes.
9. After cooking time is completed, remove the chicken breasts from Air Fryer and serve hot.

Serving Suggestions: Serve with your favourite fresh salad.
Variation Tip: You can also add tomato sauce.
Nutritional Information per Serving:
Calories: 428 | Fat: 23.5g | Sat Fat: 9.4g | Carbohydrates: 4.3g | Fibre: 1.1g | Sugar: 1.8g | Protein: 48.2g

Crispy Almond Chicken

Preparation Time: 15 minutes | **Cooking Time:** 30 minutes | **Servings:** 2

Ingredients:

- 2 chicken breast halves, boneless and skinless
- 2 small eggs
- 1 teaspoon garlic salt
- 4 tablespoons buttermilk
- 70g silvered almonds, finely chopped
- ½ teaspoon pepper

Preparation:

1. Take a shallow bowl, whisk egg, buttermilk, pepper and garlic salt.
2. Place almonds in another shallow bowl.
3. Dip chicken breasts into the egg mixture and then coat with almonds.
4. Grease basket of Ninja Foodi 2-Basket Air Fryer.
5. Press your chosen zone - "Zone 1" or "Zone 2" and then rotate the knob to select "Air Fry".
6. Set the temperature to 175 degrees C and then set the time for 5 minutes to preheat.
7. After preheating, arrange the chicken into the basket of each zone.
8. Slide the basket into the Air Fryer and set the time for 15 to 18 minutes.
9. After cooking time is completed, remove chicken from Air Fryer and serve hot.

Serving Suggestions: Serve with mashed potatoes.
Variation Tip: Fresh chicken should have a pinkish colour.
Nutritional Information per Serving:
Calories: 466 | Fat: 29.2g | Sat Fat: 3.1g | Carbohydrates: 13.3g | Fibre: 6.2g | Sugar: 4.1g | Protein: 42g

Herbed Fried Chicken

Preparation Time: 10 minutes | **Cooking Time:** 20 minutes | **Servings:** 6

Ingredients:

- 900g chicken, cut up
- 85g crushed Ritz crackers
- ½ teaspoon paprika
- ½ teaspoon garlic salt
- ½ tablespoon minced fresh parsley
- ⅛ teaspoon rubbed sage
- ⅛ teaspoon ground cumin
- ¼ teaspoon pepper
- 1 small egg, beaten

Preparation:

1. Take a bowl, add all ingredients except chicken and egg. Mix well.
2. Take another bowl and whisk egg.
3. Dip chicken in egg, then coat with cracker mixture.
4. Grease basket of Ninja Foodi 2-Basket Air Fryer.
5. Press your chosen zone - "Zone 1" or "Zone 2" and then rotate the knob to select "Air Fry".
6. Set the heat to 190 degrees C and then set the time for 5 minutes to preheat.
7. After preheating, arrange chicken into the basket of each zone.
8. Slide the basket into the Air Fryer and set the time for 15 to 20 minutes.
9. After cooking time is completed, remove the chicken from Air Fryer and place onto a platter.
10. Serve and enjoy.

Serving Suggestions: Serve alongside the steamed veggies.

Variation Tip: You can adjust the amount of spices according to your taste.

Nutritional Information per Serving:
Calories: 518 | Fat: 12.5g | Sat Fat: 3g | Carbohydrates: 5.9g | Fibre: 0.3g | Sugar: 1.3g | Protein: 90g

Sweet Potato-Crusted Chicken

Preparation Time: 10 minutes | **Cooking Time:** 10 minutes | **Servings:** 2

Ingredients:

- 225g chicken tenderloins, cut into pieces
- ½ tablespoon cornflour
- 50g sweet potato chips
- ½ teaspoon salt, divided
- 2 tablespoons plain flour
- ¼ teaspoon coarsely ground pepper
- ⅛ teaspoon baking powder

Preparation:

1. In a food processor, add chips, pepper, salt and baking powder. Pulse until ground.
2. Transfer to a shallow bowl.
3. Take a bowl, mix cornflour and remaining salt.
4. Place the chicken in the cornflour mixture and then toss with potato chip mixture.
5. Grease basket of Ninja Foodi 2-Basket Air Fryer.
6. Press your chosen zone - "Zone 1" or "Zone 2" and then rotate the knob to select "Air Fry".
7. Set the temperature to 200 degrees C and then set the time for 5 minutes to preheat.
8. After preheating, arrange chicken nuggets into the basket of each zone.
9. Slide the basket into the Air Fryer and set the time for 10 minutes.
10. After cooking time is completed, remove the chicken nuggets from Air Fryer and serve hot.

Serving Suggestions: Serve with fresh salad.

Variation Tip: You can also use breadcrumbs.

Nutritional Information per Serving:
Calories: 173 | Fat: 3.4g | Sat Fat: 0.3g | Carbohydrates: 11.6g | Fibre: 0.7g | Sugar: 0.8g | Protein: 24g

Bagel Crusted Chicken Strips

Preparation Time: 8 minutes | Cooking Time: 15 minutes | Servings: 2

Ingredients:

- 225g chicken tenderloins
- Bagel, torn
- 25g grated Parmesan cheese
- 25g panko breadcrumbs
- 30g butter, cubed
- ⅛ teaspoon crushed red pepper flakes
- ¼ teaspoon salt

Preparation:

1. Take a food processor, pulse torn bagel until crumbs are formed.
2. Place breadcrumbs in a shallow dish and add panko, cheese and pepper flakes.
3. Take another shallow bowl, microwave butter until melted.
4. Sprinkle chicken with salt.
5. Dip chicken in butter, then coat with crumb mixture.
6. Grease basket of Ninja Foodi 2-Basket Air Fryer.
7. Press your chosen zone - "Zone 1" or "Zone 2" and then rotate the knob to select "Air Fry".
8. Set the heat to 200 degrees C and then set the time for 5 minutes to preheat.
9. After preheating, arrange chicken tenderloins into the basket of each zone.
10. Slide the basket into the Air Fryer and set the time for 7 minutes.
11. While cooking, flip the chicken once halfway through.
12. After cooking time is completed, remove the chicken from Air Fryer and serve hot.

Serving Suggestions: Serve with buttery mashed potatoes.
Variation Tip: You can adjust the amount of spices according to your taste.
Nutritional Information per Serving:
Calories: 331 | Fat: 14.3g | Sat Fat: 8.3g | Carbohydrates: 16.6g | Fibre: 0.7g | Sugar: 1.5g | Protein: 27.4g

Lemony Cheese Chicken

Preparation Time: 15 minutes | Cooking Time: 25 minutes | Servings: 2

Ingredients:

- 2 chicken breast halves, boneless and skinless
- 2 tablespoons crumbled feta cheese
- ½ teaspoon dried oregano
- ¼ teaspoon pepper
- 2 tablespoons lemon juice

Preparation:

1. Take a baking dish, place chicken and pour lemon juice over chicken.
2. Sprinkle with feta cheese, oregano and pepper.
3. Press "Zone 1" of Ninja Foodi 2-Basket Air Fryer and then rotate the knob for each zone to select "Air Fry".
4. Set the heat to 200 degrees C and then set the time for 5 minutes to preheat.
5. After preheating, arrange chicken into the basket of each zone.
6. Slide the basket into the Air Fryer and set the time for 20 to 25 minutes.
7. After cooking time is completed, remove the chicken breast from Air Fryer.
8. Serve and enjoy.

Serving Suggestions: Serve alongside lemon juice.
Variation Tip: Use cheese of your choice.
Nutritional Information per Serving:
Calories: 296 | Fat: 12.5g | Sat Fat: 4.4g | Carbohydrates: 1.1g | Fibre: 0.3g | Sugar: 0.7g | Protein: 42g

Hot and Spicy Chicken

Preparation Time: 10 minutes | Cooking Time: 16 minutes | Servings: 2

Ingredients:

225g chicken breasts, skinless and boneless
½ tablespoon cayenne pepper
½ tablespoon garlic pepper seasoning
½ tablespoon sweet paprika
½ teaspoon hot sauce
55g panko breadcrumbs
2 tablespoons egg substitute
60g plain fat-free Greek yogurt

Preparation:

1. In a bowl, whisk Greek yogurt, egg substitute and hot sauce.
2. Take another bowl, mix panko breadcrumbs, paprika, garlic pepper and cayenne pepper.
3. Dip chicken strips into yogurt mixture and then coat with panko breadcrumb mixture.
4. Grease basket of Ninja Foodi 2-Basket Air Fryer.
5. Press your chosen zone - "Zone 1" or "Zone 2" and then rotate the knob to select "Air Fry".
6. Set the temperature to 200 degrees C and then set the time for 5 minutes to preheat.
7. After preheating, arrange coated chicken into the basket of each zone.
8. Slide the basket into the Air Fryer and set the time for 8 minutes per side.
9. After cooking time is completed, remove the chicken strips from Air Fryer and serve hot.

Serving Suggestions: Serve alongside hot sauce.
Variation Tip: You can also use egg whites as a substitute.
Nutritional Information per Serving:
Calories: 272 | Fat: 6.4g | Sat Fat: 2.4g | Carbohydrates: 8.1g | Fibre: 1.3g | Sugar: 1.4g | Protein: 30g

Spicy Roasted Whole Chicken

Preparation Time: 15 minutes | Cooking Time: 1 hour 10 minutes | Servings: 12

Ingredients:

115g butter, softened
4 teaspoons dried rosemary
4 teaspoons dried thyme
2 tablespoons Cajun seasoning
2 tablespoons onion powder
2 tablespoons garlic powder
2 tablespoons paprika
2 teaspoons cayenne pepper
Salt, as required
2 (1.4kg) whole chicken, neck and giblets removed

Preparation:

1. In a bowl, add the butter, herbs, spices and salt and mix well.
2. Rub each chicken with spice mixture generously.
3. With kitchen twine, tie off the wings and legs of each chicken.
4. Grease basket of Ninja Foodi 2-Basket Air Fryer.
5. Press your chosen zone - "Zone 1" or "Zone 2" and then rotate the knob to select "Bake".
6. Set the temperature to 180 degrees C and then set the time for 5 minutes to preheat.
7. After preheating, arrange 1 chicken into the basket of each zone.
8. Slide the basket into the Air Fryer and set the time for 70 minutes.
9. After cooking time is completed, remove the chickens from Air Fryer and place each onto a platter for about 10 minutes before serving.
10. Cut each chicken into desired-sized pieces and serve.

Serving Suggestions: Serve with steamed veggies.
Variation Tip: Fresh chicken should have a pinkish colour.
Nutritional Information per Serving:
Calories: 421 | Fat: 14.8g | Sat Fat: 6.9g | Carbohydrates: 2.3g | Fibre: 0.9g | Sugar: 0.5g | Protein: 66.3g

Sour and Spicy Chicken Legs

Preparation Time: 15 minutes | **Cooking Time:** 20 minutes | **Servings:** 4

Ingredients:

- 4 (200g) chicken legs
- 2 tablespoons balsamic vinegar
- 2 teaspoons garlic, minced
- Salt, as required
- 4 tablespoons plain Greek yogurt
- 1 teaspoon red chili powder
- 1 teaspoon ground cumin
- 1 teaspoon ground coriander
- Ground black pepper, as required

Preparation:

1. In a bowl, add the chicken legs, vinegar, garlic and salt and mix well.
2. Set aside for about 15 minutes.
3. Meanwhile, in another bowl, mix together the yogurt, spices, salt and black pepper.
4. Add the chicken legs into the bowl and coat with the spice mixture generously.
5. Cover the bowl of chicken and refrigerate for at least 10-12 hours.
6. Grease basket of Ninja Foodi 2-Basket Air Fryer.
7. Press your chosen zone - "Zone 1" or "Zone 2" and then rotate the knob to select "Air Fry".
8. Set the temperature to 200 degrees C and then set the time for 5 minutes to preheat.
9. After preheating, arrange 2 chicken legs into the basket of each zone.
10. Slide the basket into the Air Fryer and set the time for 20 minutes.
11. After cooking time is completed, remove the chicken legs from Air Fryer and serve hot.

Serving Suggestions: Serve alongside the orange slices.
Variation Tip: You can adjust the ratio of spices according to your taste.
Nutritional Information per Serving:
Calories: 450 | Fat: 17.2g | Sat Fat: 4.8g | Carbohydrates: 2.2g | Fibre: 0.3g | Sugar: 1.2g | Protein: 66.7g

Paprika Chicken Legs

Preparation Time: 15 minutes | **Cooking Time:** 20 minutes | **Servings:** 6

Ingredients:

- 480ml milk
- 250g flour
- 2 teaspoons garlic powder
- 2 teaspoons onion powder
- 2 teaspoons ground cumin
- 2 teaspoons paprika
- Salt and ground black pepper, as required
- 6 (200g) chicken legs

Preparation:

1. In a shallow bowl, place the milk.
2. In another shallow bowl, mix together the flour and spices.
3. Dip the chicken legs into milk and then coat with the flour mixture.
4. Repeat this process once again.
5. Grease basket of Ninja Foodi 2-Basket Air Fryer.
6. Press your chosen zone - "Zone 1" or "Zone 2" and then rotate the knob to select "Air Fry".
7. Set the temperature to 180 degrees C and then set the time for 5 minutes to preheat.
8. After preheating, arrange chicken legs in the basket of each zone.
9. Slide the basket into the Air Fryer and set the time for 25 minutes.
10. After cooking time is completed, remove the chicken legs from Air Fryer and serve hot.

Serving Suggestions: Serve with roasted veggies.
Variation Tip: Select chicken legs with a pinkish hue.
Nutritional Information per Serving:
Calories: 372 | Fat: 12.9g | Sat Fat: 3.9g | Carbohydrates: 15.5g | Fibre: 0.8g | Sugar: 0.2g | Protein: 45.4g

Honey & Mustard Glazed Chicken Drumsticks

Preparation Time: 10 minutes | Cooking Time: 20 minutes | Servings: 4

Ingredients:

- 60g Dijon mustard
- 1 tablespoon honey
- 2 tablespoons rapeseed oil
- 1 tablespoon fresh parsley, minced
- Salt and ground black pepper, as required
- 4 (150g) chicken drumsticks

Preparation:

1. In a bowl, add all ingredients except the drumsticks and mix until well combined.
2. Add the drumsticks and coat with the mixture generously.
3. Cover the bowl and place in the refrigerator to marinate overnight.
4. Grease either basket of "Zone 1" or "Zone 2" of Ninja Foodi 2-Basket Air Fryer.
5. Press your chosen zone - "Zone 1" or "Zone 2" and then rotate the knob to select "Air Fry".
6. Set the temperature to 160 degrees C and then set the time for 5 minutes to preheat.
7. After preheating, arrange drumsticks into the basket.
8. Slide basket into Air Fryer and set the time for 12 minutes.
9. After 12 minutes, flip the drumsticks and set the temperature to 200 degrees C.
10. Set the time for 8 minutes.
11. After cooking time is completed, remove the drumsticks from Air Fryer and serve hot.

Serving Suggestions: Serve with the drizzling of lime juice.

Variation Tip: You can use fresh herbs of your choice.

Nutritional Information per Serving:

Calories: 376 | Fat: 17.4g | Sat Fat: 3.1g | Carbohydrates: 5.2g | Fibre: 0.6g | Sugar: 4.5g | Protein: 47.5g

Gingered Coconut Chicken Drumsticks

Preparation Time: 10 minutes | Cooking Time: 25 minutes | Servings: 6

Ingredients:

- 120ml full-fat coconut milk
- 4 teaspoons fresh ginger, minced
- 4 teaspoons galangal, minced
- 2 teaspoons ground turmeric
- Salt, as required
- 6 (150g) chicken drumsticks

Preparation:

1. In a large bowl, place the coconut milk, galangal, ginger, and spices and mix well.
2. Add the chicken drumsticks and coat with the marinade generously.
3. Refrigerate to marinate for at least 6-8 hours.
4. Grease basket of Ninja Foodi 2-Basket Air Fryer.
5. Press your chosen zone - "Zone 1" or "Zone 2" and then rotate the knob to select "Air Fry".
6. Set the temperature to 190 degrees C and then set the time for 5 minutes to preheat.
7. After preheating, arrange 3 drumsticks into the basket of each zone.
8. Slide the basket into the Air Fryer and set the time for 25 minutes.
9. After cooking time is completed, remove the drumsticks from Air Fryer and serve hot.

Serving Suggestions: Serve with your favourite vegetables.

Variation Tip: You can use grated fresh turmeric.

Nutritional Information per Serving:

Calories: 347 | Fat: 14.8g | Sat Fat: 6.9g | Carbohydrates: 3.8g | Fibre: 1.1g | Sugar: 0.8g | Protein: 47.6g

Smoked Spicy Chicken Thighs

Preparation Time: 10 minutes | Cooking Time: 20 minutes | Servings: 8

Ingredients:

- 2 teaspoons ground cumin
- 2 teaspoons garlic powder
- 1 teaspoon smoked paprika
- 1 teaspoon ground coriander
- Salt and ground black pepper, as required
- 8 (125g) chicken thighs
- 4 tablespoons olive oil

Preparation:

1. In a large bowl, add the spices, salt and black pepper and mix well.
2. Coat the chicken thighs with oil and then rub with spice mixture.
3. Grease basket of Ninja Foodi 2-Basket Air Fryer.
4. Press your chosen zone - "Zone 1" or "Zone 2" and then rotate the knob to select "Air Fry".
5. Set the temperature to 200 degrees C and then set the time for 5 minutes to preheat.
6. After preheating, arrange 4 chicken thighs into the basket of each zone.
7. Slide the basket into the Air Fryer and set the time for 20 minutes.
8. While cooking, flip the chicken thighs once halfway through.
9. After cooking time is completed, remove the chicken thighs from Air Fryer and serve hot.

Serving Suggestions: Serve with fresh greens.
Variation Tip: Don't use chicken breasts with a faded colour.
Nutritional Information per Serving:
Calories: 334 | Fat: 17.7g | Sat Fat: 3.9g | Carbohydrates: 0.9g | Fibre: 0.2g | Sugar: 0.2g | Protein: 41.3g

Buttered Chicken Thighs

Preparation Time: 10 minutes | Cooking Time: 20 minutes | Servings: 8

Ingredients:

- 8 (100g) skinless, boneless chicken thighs
- Salt and ground black pepper, as required
- 4 tablespoons butter, melted

Preparation:

1. Line each basket of "Zone 1" and "Zone 2" of Ninja Foodi 2-Basket Air Fryer with a lightly greased square piece of foil.
2. Press your chosen zone - "Zone 1" or "Zone 2" and then rotate the knob to select "Roast".
3. Set the temperature to 230 degrees C and then set the time for 5 minutes to preheat.
4. Meanwhile, rub the chicken thighs with salt and black pepper evenly and then brush with melted butter.
5. After preheating, arrange 4 chicken thighs into the basket of each zone.
6. Slide the basket into the Air Fryer and set the time for 20 minutes.
7. After cooking time is completed, remove the chicken thighs from Air Fryer.
8. Serve hot.

Serving Suggestions: Serve alongside the lemon wedges.
Variation Tip: Use fresh chicken thighs.
Nutritional Information per Serving:
Calories: 193 | Fat: 9.8g | Sat Fat: 5.2g | Carbohydrates: 0g | Fibre: 0g | Sugar: 0g | Protein: 25.4g

Crispy Chicken Breasts with Coriander

Preparation Time: 15 minutes | Cooking Time: 40 minutes | Servings: 6

Ingredients:

- 60g flour
- 2 large eggs, beaten
- 10g fresh coriander, chopped
- 80g croutons, crushed
- 6 (125g) boneless, skinless chicken breasts

Preparation:

1. In a shallow, dish place the flour.
2. In a second shallows dish, mix together the egg and coriander.
3. In a third shallow dish, place croutons.
4. Coat the chicken breasts with flour, then dip into eggs and finally coat with croutons.
5. Grease basket of Ninja Foodi 2-Basket Air Fryer.
6. Press your chosen zone - "Zone 1" or "Zone 2" and then rotate the knob to select "Bake".
7. Set the temperature to 190 degrees C and then set the time for 5 minutes to preheat.
8. After preheating, arrange 3 chicken breasts into the basket of each zone.
9. Slide the basket into the Air Fryer and set the time for 40 minutes.
10. While cooking, flip the chicken breasts once halfway through.
11. After cooking time is completed, remove the chicken breasts from Air Fryer and serve hot.

Serving Suggestions: Serve with tomato ketchup.
Variation Tip: Coat the chicken pieces with coating evenly.
Nutritional Information per Serving:
Calories: 372 | Fat: 12.9g | Sat Fat: 3.9g | Carbohydrates: 15.5g | Fibre: 0.8g | Sugar: 0.2g | Protein: 45.4g

Parmesan Chicken Breasts with Basil

Preparation Time: 15 minutes | Cooking Time: 22 minutes | Servings: 4

Ingredients:

- 4 (150g) chicken breasts
- 2 eggs, beaten
- 200g breadcrumbs
- 2 tablespoons fresh basil
- 4 tablespoons olive oil
- 120g pasta sauce
- 50g Parmesan cheese, grated

Preparation:

1. In a shallow bowl, beat the egg.
2. In another bowl, add the oil, breadcrumbs, and basil and mix until a crumbly mixture forms.
3. Now, dip each chicken breast into the beaten egg and then coat with the breadcrumb mixture.
4. Grease basket of Ninja Foodi 2-Basket Air Fryer.
5. Press your chosen zone - "Zone 1" or "Zone 2" and then rotate the knob to select "Air Fry".
6. Set the temperature to 175 degrees C and then set the time for 5 minutes to preheat.
7. After preheating, arrange 2 chicken breasts into the basket of each zone.
8. Slide the basket into the Air Fryer and set the time for 22 minutes.
9. After 15 minutes of cooking, spoon the pasta sauce over each chicken breast, followed by the cheese.
10. After cooking time is completed, remove the chicken breasts from Air Fryer and serve hot.

Serving Suggestions: Serve with your favourite fresh salad.
Variation Tip: You can replace pasta sauce with tomato sauce too.
Nutritional Information per Serving:
Calories: 768 | Fat: 35.4g | Sat Fat: 8.8g | Carbohydrates: 457g | Fibre: 3.4g | Sugar: 6.5g | Protein: 63.9g

Cheese Chicken Cordon Bleu

Preparation Time: 15 minutes | Cooking Time: 30 minutes | Servings: 4

Ingredients:

- 4 (150g) boneless, skinless chicken breast halves, pounded into ½ cm thickness
- 4 (20g) deli ham slices
- 4 Swiss cheese slices
- 125g plain flour
- ¼ teaspoon paprika
- Salt and ground black pepper, as required
- 2 large eggs
- 4 tablespoons 2% milk
- 100g seasoned breadcrumbs
- 2 tablespoons olive oil
- 2 tablespoons butter, melted

Preparation:

1. Arrange the chicken breast halves onto a smooth surface.
2. Arrange 1 ham slice over each chicken breast half, followed by the cheese.
3. Roll up each chicken breast half and tuck in ends.
4. With toothpicks, secure the rolls.
5. In a shallow plate, mix together the flour, paprika, salt and black pepper.
6. In a shallow bowl, place the egg and milk and beat slightly.
7. In a second shallow plate, place the breadcrumbs.
8. Coat each chicken roll with flour mixture, then dip into the egg mixture and finally coat with breadcrumbs.
9. In a small frying pan, heat the oil over medium heat and cook the chicken rolls for about 3-5 minutes or until browned from all sides.
10. Grease basket of Ninja Foodi 2-Basket Air Fryer.
11. Press your chosen zone - "Zone 1" or "Zone 2" and then rotate the knob to select "Bake".
12. Set the temperature to 175 degrees C and then set the time for 5 minutes to preheat.
13. After preheating, arrange the 2 chicken rolls into the basket of each zone.
14. Slide the basket into the Air Fryer and set the time for 25 minutes.
15. After cooking time is completed, remove the baking pan of chicken from Air Fryer.
16. Transfer the chicken rolls onto a platter and discard the toothpicks.
17. Drizzle with melted butter and serve.

Serving Suggestions: Serve with mashed potatoes.
Variation Tip: Use best quality breadcrumbs.
Nutritional Information per Serving:
Calories: 672 | Fat: 28g | Sat Fat: 12g | Carbohydrates: 45.4g | Fibre: 2.4g | Sugar: 3.4g | Protein: 56.2g

Cheese & Spinach Stuffed Chicken

Preparation Time: 15 minutes | Cooking Time: 30 minutes | Servings: 4

Ingredients:

- 2 tablespoon olive oil
- 85g fresh spinach
- 125g ricotta cheese, shredded
- 4 (100g) skinless, boneless chicken breasts
- Salt and ground black pepper, as required
- 4 tablespoons Parmesan cheese, grated
- ½ teaspoon paprika

Preparation:

1. In a medium frying pan, heat the oil over medium heat and cook the spinach for about 3-4 minutes.
2. Stir in the ricotta and cook for about 40-60 seconds.
3. Remove the frying pan from heat and set aside to cool.
4. Cut slits into the chicken breasts about ½ cm apart but not all the way through.
5. Stuff each chicken breast with the spinach mixture.
6. Season each chicken breast with salt and black pepper and then sprinkle the top with Parmesan cheese and paprika.
7. Grease basket of Ninja Foodi 2-Basket Air Fryer.
8. Press your chosen zone - "Zone 1" or "Zone 2" and then rotate the knob to select "Air Fry".
9. Set the temperature to 200 degrees C and then set the time for 5 minutes to preheat.
10. After preheating, arrange 2 chicken breasts into the basket of each zone.
11. Slide the basket into the Air Fryer and set the time for 25 minutes.
12. After cooking time is completed, remove the chicken breasts from Air Fryer and serve hot.

Serving Suggestions: Serve with fresh salad.
Variation Tip: You can use kale instead of spinach.
Nutritional Information per Serving:
Calories: 272 | Fat: 15g | Sat Fat: 5g | Carbohydrates: 2.8g | Fibre: 0.7g | Sugar: 0.2g | Protein: 31.5g

Rosemary Lime Turkey Legs

Preparation Time: 10 minutes | **Cooking Time:** 30 minutes | **Servings:** 4

▶ Ingredients:

4 garlic cloves, minced
2 tablespoons fresh rosemary, minced
2 teaspoons fresh lime zest, finely grated
4 tablespoons olive oil
2 tablespoons fresh lime juice
Salt and ground black pepper, as required
4 turkey legs

▶ Preparation:

1. In a large baking dish, mix together the garlic, rosemary, lime zest, oil, lime juice, salt, and black pepper.
2. Add the turkey legs and generously coat with marinade.
3. Refrigerate to marinate for about 6-8 hours.
4. Grease basket of Ninja Foodi 2-Basket Air Fryer.
5. Press your chosen zone - "Zone 1" or "Zone 2" and then rotate the knob to select "Air Fry".
6. Set the temperature to 175 degrees C and then set the time for 5 minutes to preheat.
7. After preheating, arrange 2 turkey legs into the basket of each zone.
8. Slide the basket into the Air Fryer and set the time for 30 minutes.
9. While cooking, flip the turkey legs once halfway through.
10. After cooking time is completed, remove the turkey legs from Air Fryer and serve hot.

Serving Suggestions: Serve with buttery mashed potatoes.
Variation Tip: Try to use fresh turkey legs.
Nutritional Information per Serving:
Calories: 709 | Fat: 32.7g | Sat Fat: 7.8g | Carbohydrates: 2.3g | Fibre: 0.9g | Sugar: 0.1g | Protein: 97.2g

Simple Baked Turkey Breast

Preparation Time: 10 minutes | **Cooking Time:** 1 hour 20 minutes | **Servings:** 12

▶ Ingredients:

2 (1.2kg) bone-in, skin-on turkey breast half
Salt and ground black pepper, as required

▶ Preparation:

1. Rub the turkey breast with the salt and black pepper evenly.
2. Grease basket of Ninja Foodi 2-Basket Air Fryer.
3. Press your chosen zone - "Zone 1" or "Zone 2" and then rotate the knob to select "Bake".
4. Set the temperature to 200 degrees C and then set the time for 5 minutes to preheat.
5. After preheating, arrange 1 turkey breast into the basket of each zone.
6. Slide the basket into the Air Fryer and set the time for 80 minutes.
7. After cooking time is completed, remove the turkey breasts from Air Fryer and place onto a platter.
8. With a piece of foil, cover each turkey breast for about 20 minutes before slicing.
9. With a sharp knife, cut each turkey breast into desired size slices and serve.

Serving Suggestions: Serve alongside the steamed veggies.
Variation Tip: Avoid using turkey breast with flat spots.
Nutritional Information per Serving:
Calories: 326 | Fat: 14.6g | Sat Fat: 4g | Carbohydrates: 0g | Fibre: 0g | Sugar: 0g | Protein: 45.6g

Garlicky Herbed Duck Legs

Preparation Time: 10 minutes | **Cooking Time:** 30 minutes | **Servings:** 4

Ingredients:

- 4 garlic cloves, minced
- 2 tablespoons fresh parsley, chopped
- 2 teaspoons five-spice powder
- Salt and ground black pepper, as required
- 4 duck legs

Preparation:

1. In a bowl, add the garlic, parsley, five-spice powder, salt and black pepper and mix until well combined.
2. Rub the duck legs with garlic mixture generously.
3. Grease basket of Ninja Foodi 2-Basket Air Fryer.
4. Press your chosen zone - "Zone 1" or "Zone 2" and then rotate the knob to select "Air Fry".
5. Set the temperature to 170 degrees C and then set the time for 5 minutes to preheat.
6. After preheating, arrange 2 duck legs into the basket of each zone.
7. Slide the basket into the Air Fryer and set the time for 30 minutes.
8. After cooking time is completed, remove the duck legs from Air Fryer and serve hot.

Serving Suggestions: Serve alongside the fresh salad.
Variation Tip: Make sure that the skin of duck legs is clear and soft.
Nutritional Information per Serving:
Calories: 434 | Fat: 14.4g | Sat Fat: 0g | Carbohydrates: 1.1g | Fibre: 0.1g | Sugar: 0.1g | Protein: 704

Chapter 6 Beef, Pork & Lamb Recipes

Easy Lamb Steak

Preparation Time: 2 minutes | Cooking Time: 7 minutes | Servings: 2

Ingredients:

2 lamb steaks
½ teaspoon salt
Drizzle of olive oil
½ teaspoon ground black pepper

Preparation:

1. Take a bowl, add every ingredient except lamb steak. Mix well.
2. Rub lamb steaks with a little olive oil.
3. Press each side of steak into salt and pepper mixture.
4. Grease basket of Ninja Foodi 2-Basket Air Fryer.
5. Press your chosen zone - "Zone 1" or "Zone 2" and then rotate the knob to select "Air Fry".
6. Set the heat to 200 degrees C and then set the time for 5 minutes to preheat.
7. After preheating, arrange steak into the basket of each zone.
8. Slide the basket into the Air Fryer and set the time for 5 minutes.
9. While cooking, flip the steak once halfway through and cook for more 5 minutes.
10. After cooking time is completed, remove it from Air Fryer and place onto a platter for about 10 minutes before slicing.
11. With a sharp knife, cut each steak into desired-sized slices and serve.

Serving Suggestions: Serve with mashed potatoes.
Variation Tip: Feel free to use the seasoning of your choice.
Nutritional Information per Serving:
Calories: 190 | Fat: 7.4g | Sat Fat: 2.4g | Carbohydrates: 3.7g | Fibre: 1.5g | Sugar: 2.6g | Protein: 24.8g

Simple Beef Roast

Preparation Time: 10 minutes | Cooking Time: 50 minutes | Servings: 8

Ingredients:

1 (455g) beef roast
Salt and ground black
pepper, as required

Preparation:

1. Grease either basket "Zone 1" or "Zone 2" of Ninja Foodi 2-Basket Air Fryer.
2. Press your chosen zone - "Zone 1" or "Zone 2" and then rotate the knob for the zone to select "Roast".
3. Set the temperature to 175 degrees C and then set the time for 5 minutes to preheat.
4. Rub roast with salt and black pepper generously.
5. After preheating, arrange the roast into the basket.
6. Slide basket into Air Fryer and set the time for 50 minutes.
7. After cooking time is completed, remove roast from Air Fryer and place onto a platter for about 10 minutes before slicing.
8. With a sharp knife, cut roast into desired-sized slices and serve.

Serving Suggestions: Serve with lemon wedges.
Variation Tip: Feel free to use the seasoning of your choice.
Nutritional Information per Serving:
Calories: 105 | Fat: 3.5g | Sat Fat: 1.3g | Carbohydrates: 0g | Fibre: 0g | Sugar: 0g | Protein: 17.2g

Bacon Wrapped Filet Mignon

Preparation Time: 10 minutes | Cooking Time: 15 minutes | Servings: 2

▶ Ingredients:

2 (50g) filet mignon
2 bacon slices
Olive oil cooking spray
Salt and ground black pepper, as required

▶ Preparation:

1. Wrap 1 bacon slice around each filet mignon and secure with toothpicks.
2. Season the filets with salt and black pepper lightly.
3. Grease basket of Ninja Foodi 2-Basket Air Fryer.
4. Press your chosen zone - "Zone 1" or "Zone 2" and then rotate the knob to select "Air Fry".
5. Set the temperature to 200 degrees C and then set the time for 5 minutes to preheat.
6. After preheating, arrange the filets into the basket of each zone.
7. Slide the basket into the Air Fryer and set the time for 15 minutes.
8. While cooking, flip the filets once halfway through.
9. After cooking time is completed, remove the filets from Air Fryer and serve hot.

Serving Suggestions: Serve alongside the greens.
Variation Tip: Don't use the filets that are less than 4 cm thick.
Nutritional Information per Serving:
Calories: 204 | Fat: 11.7g | Sat Fat: 4g | Carbohydrates: 0.3g | Fibre: 0g | Sugar: 0g | Protein: 23g

Delicious BBQ Pork Loin

Preparation Time: 10 minutes | Cooking Time: 30 minutes | Servings: 6

▶ Ingredients:

1 (455g) pork loin
2-3 tablespoons barbecue
seasoning rub
2 tablespoons olive oil

▶ Preparation:

1. Coat pork loin with oil and then rub with barbecue seasoning rub generously.
2. Grease either basket "Zone 1" or "Zone 2" of Ninja Foodi 2-Basket Air Fryer.
3. Press your chosen zone - "Zone 1" or "Zone 2" and then rotate the knob for each zone to select "Bake".
4. Set the temperature to 175 degrees C for the zone and then set the time for 5 minutes to preheat.
5. After preheating, arrange pork loin into the basket.
6. Slide basket into Air Fryer and set the time for 30 minutes.
7. After cooking time is completed, remove pork loin from Air Fryer and place onto a platter for about 10 minutes before slicing.
8. With a sharp knife, cut pork loin into desired-sized slices and serve.

Serving Suggestions: Serve alongside the roasted veggies.
Variation Tip: You can use the seasoning of your choice.
Nutritional Information per Serving:
Nutritional Value:
Calories: 238 | Fat: 15.2g | Sat Fat: 4.6g | Carbohydrates: 2g | Fibre: 0g | Sugar: 0g | Protein: 20.7g

Sweet BBQ Pork Ribs

Preparation Time: 15 minutes | Cooking Time: 26 minutes | Servings: 4

▶ **Ingredients:**

900g pork ribs
85g honey, divided
240g BBQ sauce
½ teaspoon garlic powder
2 tablespoons tomato ketchup
1 tablespoon Worcestershire sauce
1 tablespoon low-sodium soy sauce
Freshly ground white pepper, as required

▶ **Preparation:**

1. In a bowl, mix together honey and the remaining ingredients except pork ribs.
2. Add the pork ribs and coat with the mixture generously.
3. Refrigerate to marinate for about 20 minutes.
4. Grease basket of Ninja Foodi 2-Basket Air Fryer.
5. Press your chosen zone - "Zone 1" or "Zone 2" and then rotate the knob to select "Air Fry".
6. Set the temperature to 180 degrees C and then set the time for 5 minutes to preheat.
7. After preheating, arrange the ribs into the basket of each zone.
8. Slide the basket into the Air Fryer and set the time for 26 minutes.
9. While cooking, flip the ribs once halfway through.
10. After cooking time is completed, remove the ribs from Air Fryer and place onto serving plates.
11. Drizzle with the remaining honey and serve immediately.

Serving Suggestions: Serve with steamed veggies.
Variation Tip: You can use BBQ sauce of your choice.
Nutritional Information per Serving:
Calories: 791 | Fat: 40.4g | Sat Fat: 14.3g | Carbohydrates: 43.3g | Fibre: 0.5g | Sugar: 36.5g | Protein: 60.6g

Air Fried New York Strip Steak

Preparation Time: 10 minutes | Cooking Time: 10 minutes | Servings: 2

▶ **Ingredients:**

1 (110g) New York strip steaks
1½ teaspoons olive oil
Salt and ground black pepper, as required

▶ **Preparation:**

1. Grease either basket of "Zone 1" and "Zone 2" in Ninja Foodi 2-Basket Air Fryer.
2. Press your chosen zone - "Zone 1" or "Zone 2" and then rotate the knob for each zone to select "Air Fry".
3. Set the temperature to 200 degrees C for the zone and then set the time for 5 minutes to preheat.
4. Coat the steaks with oil and then sprinkle with salt and black pepper evenly.
5. After preheating, arrange the steak into the basket.
6. Slide basket into Air Fryer and set the time for 10 minutes.
7. While cooking, flip the steak once halfway through.
8. After cooking time is completed, remove the steak from Air Fryer and place onto a platter for about 10 minutes.
9. Cut steak into desired size slices and serve immediately.

Serving Suggestions: Serve with fresh baby kale.
Variation Tip: Season the steaks with salt and black pepper generously.
Nutritional Information per Serving:
Calories: 809 | Fat: 56.3g | Sat Fat: 18.9g | Carbohydrates: 0g | Fibre: 0g | Sugar: 0g | Protein: 77.7g

Bacon Wrapped Hot Dogs

Preparation Time: 10 minutes | Cooking Time: 15 minutes | Servings: 2

▶ Ingredients:

2 bacon strips
2 hot dogs
Salt and black pepper, to taste

▶ Preparation:

1. Wrap each hot dog with bacon strip and season with salt and black pepper.
2. Grease basket of Ninja Foodi 2-Basket Air Fryer.
3. Press your chosen zone - "Zone 1" or "Zone 2" and then rotate the knob to select "Air Fry".
4. Set the temperature to 200 degrees C and then set the time for 5 minutes to preheat.
5. After preheating, arrange bacon wrapped hot dogs into the basket of each zone.
6. Slide the basket into the Air Fryer and set the time for 15 minutes.
7. While cooking, flip the hot dogs once halfway through.
8. After cooking time is completed, remove the filets from Air Fryer and serve hot.

Serving Suggestions: Serve alongside the green beans.
Variation Tip: Black pepper can be replaced with cayenne pepper.
Nutritional Information per Serving:
Calories: 242 | Fat: 21.7g | Sat Fat: 8g | Carbohydrates: 1.8g | Fibre: 0g | Sugar: 1.5g | Protein: 8.8g

Seasoned Steak

Preparation Time: 10 minutes | Cooking Time: 30 minutes | Servings: 6

▶ Ingredients:

1 (455g) flank steaks
1½ tablespoons taco
seasoning rub

▶ Preparation:

1. Grease either basket of "Zone 1" or "Zone 2" of Ninja Foodi 2-Basket Air Fryer.
2. Press your chosen zone - "Zone 1" or "Zone 2" and then rotate the knob for the zone to select "Bake".
3. Set the temperature to 215 degrees C and then set the time for 5 minutes to preheat.
4. Rub the steaks with taco seasoning evenly.
5. After preheating, arrange the steak into the basket.
6. Slide basket into Air Fryer and set the time for 30 minutes.
7. After cooking time is completed, remove the steaks from Air Fryer and place onto a cutting board for about 10-15 minutes before slicing.
8. With a sharp knife, cut steak into desired size slices and serve.

Serving Suggestions: Serve alongside salad.
Variation Tip: Choose the steak that is uniform in thickness.
Nutritional Information per Serving:
Calories: 174 | Fat: 6.3g | Sat Fat: 2.6g | Carbohydrates: 5.5g | Fibre: 0g | Sugar: 1.4g | Protein: 21g

Herbed Pork Chops

Preparation Time: 15 minutes | **Cooking Time:** 12 minutes | **Servings:** 2

Ingredients:

- 2 (75g) (2.5cm thick) pork chops
- 2 tablespoons olive oil
- 1 tablespoon Dijon mustard
- ½ tablespoon ground coriander
- 1 teaspoon sugar
- 2 garlic cloves, minced
- ½ tablespoon fresh coriander, chopped
- ½ tablespoon fresh rosemary, chopped
- ½ tablespoon fresh parsley, chopped
- Salt, as required

Preparation:

1. In a bowl, mix together the garlic, herbs, oil, mustard, coriander, sugar, and salt.
2. Add the pork chops and coat with marinade generously.
3. Cover and refrigerate for about 2-3 hours.
4. Remove the chops from the refrigerator. Set aside at room temperature for about 30 minutes before cooking.
5. Grease either basket of "Zone 1" or "Zone 2" of Ninja Foodi 2-Basket Air Fryer.
6. Press your chosen zone - "Zone 1" or "Zone 2" and then rotate the knob for each zone to select "Air Fry".
7. Set the temperature to 200 degrees C for the zone and then set the time for 5 minutes to preheat.
8. After preheating, arrange pork chops into the basket.
9. Slide basket into Air Fryer and set the time for 12 minutes.
10. After cooking time is completed, remove the chops from Air Fryer.
11. Serve hot.

Serving Suggestions: Serve with your favourite dipping sauce.

Variation Tip: Look for chops that are pinkish-red in colour.

Nutritional Information per Serving:
Calories: 413 | Fat: 35.6g | Sat Fat: 10g | Carbohydrates: 4g | Fibre: 0.7g | Sugar: 2.1g | Protein: 19.7g

Garlicky Lamb Loin Chops

Preparation Time: 10 minutes | **Cooking Time:** 13 minutes | **Servings:** 2

Ingredients:

- 4 (50g, 1 cm thick) lamb loin chops
- 2 garlic cloves, crushed
- 1 teaspoon chili powder
- 2 teaspoons fresh rosemary, minced
- Salt and ground black pepper, as required

Preparation:

1. In a large bowl, place all ingredients and mix well.
2. Refrigerate to marinate overnight.
3. Remove chops from bowl and season with a little salt.
4. Grease either basket of "Zone 1" or "Zone 2" of Ninja Foodi 2-Basket Air Fryer.
5. Press your chosen zone - "Zone 1" or "Zone 2" and then rotate the knob for the zone to select "Bake".
6. Set the temperature to 200 degrees C and then set the time for 5 minutes to preheat.
7. Rub the lamb chops with salt and black pepper generously.
8. After preheating, arrange lamb chops into the basket.
9. Slide basket into Air Fryer and set the time for 11 minutes.
10. Flip the chops once halfway through.
11. After cooking time is completed, remove the chops from Air Fryer and serve hot.

Serving Suggestions: Serve with the drizzling of lemon juice.

Variation Tip: Don't undercook the lamb chops.

Nutritional Information per Serving:
Calories: 223 | Fat: 8.7g | Sat Fat: 3.1g | Carbohydrates: 2.5g | Fibre: 1g | Sugar: 0.1g | Protein: 32.3g

Cinnamon Lamb Meatballs

Preparation Time: 10 minutes | **Cooking Time:** 12 minutes | **Servings:** 4

Ingredients:

- 455g lamb mince
- 1 teaspoon ground cinnamon
- 1 teaspoon ground cumin
- 2 teaspoons granulated onion
- 2 tablespoons fresh parsley
- Salt and black pepper, to taste

Preparation:

1. Add lamb mince, onion, cinnamon, cumin, parsley, salt and pepper in a large bowl. Mix until well combined.
2. Make 2.5cm balls from the mixture and set aside.
3. Grease basket of Ninja Foodi 2-Basket Air Fryer.
4. Press your chosen zone - "Zone 1" or "Zone 2" and then rotate the knob to select "Air Fry".
5. Set the temperature to 195 degrees C and then set the time for 5 minutes to preheat.
6. After preheating, arrange the meatballs into the basket of each zone.
7. Slide the basket into the Air Fryer and set the time for 12 minutes.
8. Flip the meatballs once halfway through.
9. Take out and serve warm.

Serving Suggestions: Serve with the garnishing of sesame seeds.
Variation Tip: Strictly follow the ratio of ingredients.
Nutritional Information per Serving:
Calories: 215 | Fat: 8.5g | Sat Fat: 3g | Carbohydrates: 0.8g | Fibre: 0.4g | Sugar: 0g | Protein: 32g

Delicious Cajun Flank Steak

Preparation Time: 10 minutes | **Cooking Time:** 7 minutes | **Servings:** 4

Ingredients:

- 900g flank steak
- 1 Cajun seasoning
- ½ teaspoon smoked paprika
- Salt, to taste

Preparation:

1. Grease either basket of "Zone 1" or "Zone 2" of Ninja Foodi 2-Basket Air Fryer.
2. Press your chosen zone - "Zone 1" or "Zone 2" and then rotate the knob for the zone to select "Bake".
3. Set the temperature to 215 degrees C and then set the time for 5 minutes to preheat.
4. Rub the steaks with Cajun seasoning evenly.
5. After preheating, arrange steak into the basket.
6. Slide basket into Air Fryer and set the time for 7 minutes.
7. After cooking time is completed, remove the steak from Air Fryer and set aside to cool.
8. Slice and serve.

Serving Suggestions: Serve with fresh baby greens.
Variation Tip: Taco seasoning can also be used.
Nutritional Information per Serving:
Calories: 441 | Fat: 18.9g | Sat Fat: 7.8g | Carbohydrates: 0.1g | Fibre: 0.1g | Sugar: 0g | Protein: 63.1g

Herbed Lamb Chops

Preparation Time: 5 minutes | Cooking Time: 10 minutes | Servings: 2

Ingredients:

225g lamb, pre-cut chops
1 tablespoon olive oil
1 teaspoon fresh rosemary
½ teaspoon fresh minced
½ teaspoon thyme
garlic
¼ teaspoon salt
¼ teaspoon pepper

Preparation:

1. Take a bowl, add oil, thyme, garlic, salt, pepper and rosemary. Mix well.
2. Add in lamb chops and toss to coat well.
3. Continue until we have a chops well coated with seasonings.
4. Grease either basket of "Zone 1" or "Zone 2" of Ninja Foodi 2-Basket Air Fryer.
5. Press your chosen zone - "Zone 1" or "Zone 2" and then rotate the knob for the zone to select "Bake".
6. Set the heat to 195 degrees C and then set the time for 5 minutes to preheat.
7. After preheating, arrange lamb chops into the basket.
8. Slide basket into Air Fryer and set the time for 10 to 15 minutes.
9. While cooking, flip the lamb chops once halfway through.
10. After cooking time is completed, remove the lamb chops from Air Fryer and serve hot.

Serving Suggestions: Serve alongside the greens.
Variation Tip: Thickness of chops may affect cooking time
Nutritional Information per Serving:
Calories: 275 | Fat: 15.4g | Sat Fat: 4g | Carbohydrates: 0.9g | Fibre: 0.4g | Sugar: 0g | Protein: 32g

Easy Baked Lamb Steaks

Preparation Time: 2 minutes | Cooking Time: 7 minutes | Servings: 2

Ingredients:

2 lamb steaks
½ teaspoon salt
½ teaspoon ground black
pepper
Drizzle of olive oil

Preparation:

1. Take a bowl, add every ingredient except lamb steak. Mix well.
2. Rub lamb steaks with a little olive oil.
3. Press each side of steak into salt and pepper mixture.
4. Grease either basket of "Zone 1" or "Zone 2" of Ninja Foodi 2-Basket Air Fryer.
5. Press your chosen zone - "Zone 1" or "Zone 2" and then rotate the knob for the zone to select "Bake".
6. Set the heat to 200 degrees C and then set the time for 5 minutes to preheat.
7. After preheating, arrange steak into the basket.
8. Slide basket into Air Fryer and set the time for 5 minutes.
9. While cooking, flip the steak once halfway through and cook for more 5 minutes.
10. After cooking time is completed, remove it from Air Fryer and place onto a platter for about 10 minutes before slicing.
11. With a sharp knife, cut steak into desired-sized slices and serve.

Serving Suggestions: Serve with lemon wedges.
Variation Tip: Feel free to use the seasoning of your choice.
Nutritional Information per Serving:
Calories: 159 | Fat: 6.3g | Sat Fat: 2.2g | Carbohydrates: 0.3g | Fibre: 0.1g | Sugar: 0g | Protein: 23.9g

Herbed Beef Roast

Preparation Time: 15 minutes | **Cooking Time:** 35 minutes | **Servings:** 3

Ingredients:

- 455g beef roast
- ½ onion, chopped
- 1 teaspoon dried rosemary
- 1 teaspoon dried thyme
- ½ tablespoon olive oil
- Salt, to taste

Preparation:

1. Grease either basket of "Zone 1" or "Zone 2" of Ninja Foodi 2-Basket Air Fryer.
2. Press your chosen zone - "Zone 1" or "Zone 2" and then rotate the knob for the zone to select "Bake".
3. Set the temperature to 175 degrees C and then set the time for 5 minutes to preheat.
4. Add salt, rosemary, thyme and olive oil in a bowl. Mix well.
5. Rub the mixture on the roast and set aside.
6. After preheating, place onion and arrange roast into the basket.
7. Slide basket into Air Fryer and set the time for 35 minutes.
8. After cooking time is completed, remove roast from Air Fryer and place onto a platter.
9. Slice and serve.

Serving Suggestions: Serve with melted butter on the top.
Variation Tip: Fresh rosemary can also be used.
Nutritional Information per Serving:
Calories: 310 | Fat: 11.9g | Sat Fat: 3.9g | Carbohydrates: 2.2g | Fibre: 0.7g | Sugar: 0.8g | Protein: 46.1g

BBQ Baby Back Ribs

Preparation Time: 10 minutes | **Cooking Time:** 30 minutes | **Servings:** 6

Ingredients:

- 1 rack baby back ribs
- 240g BBQ sauce
- 90g BBQ rub
- 240ml water

Preparation:

1. In a bowl, mix together BBQ sauce, BBQ rub and water.
2. Add the pork ribs and coat with the mixture generously.
3. Refrigerate to marinate for about 20 minutes.
4. Grease basket of Ninja Foodi 2-Basket Air Fryer.
5. Press your chosen zone - "Zone 1" or "Zone 2" and then rotate the knob to select "Air Fry".
6. Set the temperature to 180 degrees C and then set the time for 5 minutes to preheat.
7. After preheating, arrange the ribs into the basket of each zone.
8. Slide the basket into the Air Fryer and set the time for 30 minutes.
9. While cooking, flip the ribs once halfway through.
10. After cooking time is completed, remove the ribs from Air Fryer and place onto serving plates.
11. Serve and enjoy!

Serving Suggestions: Serve with honey on the top.
Variation Tip: You can use BBQ sauce of your choice.
Nutritional Information per Serving:
Calories: 177 | Fat: 6.1g | Sat Fat: 2.1g | Carbohydrates: 13.7g | Fibre: 0.4g | Sugar: 7.4g | Protein: 26g

Baked Pork Chops with Herbs

Preparation Time: 10 minutes | Cooking Time: 8 minutes | Servings: 4

Ingredients:

- 4 pork chops
- 2 tablespoons parsley
- 2 tablespoons thyme
- 4 tablespoons paprika
- 2 tablespoons basil
- 2 tablespoons oregano
- 2 tablespoons olive oil
- Salt, to taste

Preparation:

1. Add parsley, thyme, paprika, basil, oregano, salt and olive oil in a large bowl. Mix well.
2. Add pork chops in the bowl and coat with marinade generously.
3. Cover and refrigerate for about 2-3 hours.
4. Remove the chops from the refrigerator and set aside at room temperature for about 30 minutes before cooking.
5. Grease either basket of "Zone 1" or "Zone 2" of Ninja Foodi 2-Basket Air Fryer.
6. Press your chosen zone - "Zone 1" or "Zone 2" and then rotate the knob for the zone to select "Bake".
7. Set the heat to 200 degrees C and then set the time for 5 minutes to preheat.
8. After preheating, arrange 4 chops into the basket.
9. Slide basket into Air Fryer and set the time for 8 minutes.
10. After cooking time is completed, remove the chops from Air Fryer.
11. Serve hot.

Serving Suggestions: Serve with your chopped mint leaves on the top.
Variation Tip: Coconut oil can also be used instead of olive oil.
Nutritional Information per Serving:
Calories: 348 | Fat: 28.1g | Sat Fat: 8.7g | Carbohydrates: 6.3g | Fibre: 4.1g | Sugar: 0.8g | Protein: 19.5g

Pork Tenderloin

Preparation Time: 10 minutes | Cooking Time: 20 minutes | Servings: 8

Ingredients:

- 1.8kg pork tenderloin
- 2 tablespoons Cajun
- seasoning
- Salt and pepper, to taste

Preparation:

1. Add Cajun seasoning, salt and pepper in a large bowl. Mix well.
2. Add pork tenderloin in it and toss to coat well.
3. Grease basket of Ninja Foodi 2-Basket Air Fryer.
4. Press your chosen zone - "Zone 1" or "Zone 2" and then rotate the knob to select "Bake".
5. Set the heat to 175 degrees C and then set the time for 5 minutes to preheat.
6. After preheating, arrange pork tenderloin into the basket of each zone.
7. Slide the basket into the Air Fryer and set the time for 20 minutes.
8. After cooking time is completed, remove pork tenderloin from Air Fryer and place onto a plate.
9. Slice each pork tenderloin and serve.

Serving Suggestions: Serve alongside the boiled vegetables.
Variation Tip: You can also use taco seasoning.
Nutritional Information per Serving:
Calories: 324 | Fat: 8g | Sat Fat: 2.7g | Carbohydrates: 0g | Fibre: 0g | Sugar: 0g | Protein: 59.4g

Bacon Wrapped Pork Tenderloin

Preparation Time: 15 minutes | Cooking Time: 20 minutes | Servings: 12

Ingredients:

- 2 (900g) pork tenderloins
- 12 bacon strips
- ½ teaspoon ground black pepper
- Salt, to taste

Preparation:

1. Season pork tenderloins with salt and pepper and set aside.
2. Wrap pork tenderloin with bacon strips and set aside for a while.
3. Grease basket of Ninja Foodi 2-Basket Air Fryer.
4. Press your chosen zone - "Zone 1" or "Zone 2" and then rotate the knob to select "Air Fry".
5. Set the heat to 180 degrees C and then set the time for 5 minutes to preheat.
6. After preheating, arrange bacon wrapped pork tenderloins into the basket of each zone.
7. Slide the basket into the Air Fryer and set the time for 20 minutes.
8. After cooking time is completed, remove bacon wrapped pork tenderloins from Air Fryer and place on a plate.
9. Slice and serve.

Serving Suggestions: Serve with fresh parsley on the top.
Variation Tip: Chili flakes can be used for spicy taste.
Nutritional Information per Serving:
Calories: 556 | Fat: 27.4g | Sat Fat: 9.7g | Carbohydrates: 0.1g | Fibre: 0.1g | Sugar: 0g | Protein: 71.7g

Simple Seasoned Lamb Chops

Preparation Time: 10 minutes | Cooking Time: 10 minutes | Servings: 2

Ingredients:

- 2 lamb chops
- 2 tablespoons taco seasoning
- Salt and pepper, to taste

Preparation:

1. Grease either basket of "Zone 1" or "Zone 2" of Ninja Foodi 2-Basket Air Fryer.
2. Press your chosen zone - "Zone 1" or "Zone 2" and then rotate the knob for the zone to select "Bake".
3. Set the temperature to 190 degrees C and then set the time for 5 minutes to preheat.
4. Rub the lamb chops generously with salt, black pepper and taco seasoning.
5. After preheating, arrange lamb chop into the basket.
6. Slide basket into Air Fryer and set the time for 10 minutes.
7. After cooking time is completed, remove the chops from Air Fryer and serve hot.

Serving Suggestions: Serve with chopped mint leaves.
Variation Tip: Lemon juice can also be added to enhance taste.
Nutritional Information per Serving:
Calories: 729 | Fat: 37.8g | Sat Fat: 19.7g | Carbohydrates: 41.1g | Fibre: 0g | Sugar: 0g | Protein: 55.7g

Chapter 7 Dessert Recipes

Oreo Muffins

Preparation Time: 10 minutes | Cooking Time: 10 minutes | Servings: 3

Ingredients:

120ml milk
½ pack Oreo biscuits, crushed
½ teaspoon cocoa powder
½ teaspoon baking soda
¼ teaspoon baking powder

Preparation:

1. Take a bowl, add milk, cocoa powder, baking soda, biscuits and baking powder. Mix them well.
2. Place the mixture into prepared muffin cups evenly.
3. Line each basket of "Zone 1" and "Zone 2" with parchment paper.
4. Press your chosen zone - "Zone 1" or "Zone 2" and then rotate the knob to select "Air Fry".
5. Set the temperature to 160 degrees C and then set the time for 5 minutes to preheat.
6. After preheating, arrange the muffin cups into the basket.
7. Slide the basket into the Air Fryer and set the time for 10 minutes.
8. After cooking time is completed, remove the muffin cups from Air Fryer.
9. Refrigerate.
10. Serve and enjoy!

Serving Suggestions: Serve with the topping of whipped cream.
Variation Tip: Refrigerate before serving.
Nutritional Information per Serving:
Calories: 165 | Fat: 7.4g | Sat Fat: 4.7g | Carbohydrates: 21g | Fibre: 0.3g | Sugar: 16g | Protein: 4.6g

Lemony Cheesecake

Preparation Time: 8 minutes | Cooking Time: 25 minutes | Servings: 2

Ingredients:

615g ricotta cheese
2 eggs
1 tablespoon fresh lemon juice
3 tablespoons corn flour
2 teaspoon vanilla extract
1 teaspoon fresh lemon zest, finely grated

Preparation:

1. Press either "Zone 1" or "Zone 2" and then rotate the knob to select "Bake".
2. Set the temperature to 160 degrees C and then set the time for 5 minutes to preheat.
3. Take a bowl, mix together all the ingredients.
4. Place the mixture into a baking dish.
5. After preheating, arrange baking dish into the basket.
6. Slide basket into Air Fryer and set the time for 25 minutes.
7. After cooking time is completed, remove from the Air Fryer.
8. Set aside to cool.
9. Serve and enjoy!

Serving Suggestions: Garnish with icing sugar.
Variation Tip: Refrigerate before using.
Nutritional Information per Serving:
Calories: 558 | Fat: 29g | Sat Fat: 16.7g | Carbohydrates: 30.7g | Fibre: 0.1g | Sugar: 2.1g | Protein: 40.9g

Oatmeal Butter Cookies

Preparation Time: 10 minutes | Cooking Time: 7 minutes | Servings: 20

Ingredients:

200g brown sugar
100g granulated sugar
230g butter, melted
2 large eggs
2 teaspoons vanilla extract
125g plain flour
1 teaspoon baking soda
1 teaspoon cinnamon
¾ teaspoon salt
250g rolled oats

Preparation:

1. In a mixing dish, combine both sugars and melted butter. Blend until everything is well combined.
2. Combine the eggs and vanilla extract in a mixing bowl. Beat the drums thoroughly.
3. Sift the flour, baking soda, cinnamon, and salt over the top and whisk until everything is thoroughly combined.
4. Add the rolled oats and mix well.
5. Line the baskets of your Air Fryer with parchment paper.
6. Press your chosen zone - "Zone 1" or "Zone 2" and then rotate the knob to select "Air Fryer".
7. Set the temperature to 150 degrees C, and then set the time for 5 minutes to preheat.
8. After preheating, fill the Air Fryer basket with walnut-sized cookie dough balls of each zone.
9. Slide the baskets into Air Fryer and set the time for 7 minutes.
10. After cooking time is completed, transfer onto serving plates and serve.

Serving Suggestions: Top with chocolate syrup.
Variation Tip: You can skip the cinnamon.
Nutritional Information per Serving:
Calories: 132 | Fat: 7g | Sat Fat: 4g | Carbohydrates: 2g | Fibre: 2g | Sugar: 9g | Protein: 4g

Chocolate Cake

Preparation Time: 12 minutes | Cooking Time: 25 minutes | Servings: 6

Ingredients:

3 eggs
120g sour cream
115g butter, softened
2 teaspoon vanilla extract
10 tablespoons sugar
125g flour
1 teaspoon baking powder
5 tablespoons cocoa powder
½ teaspoon baking soda
A pinch of salt

Preparation:

1. Take a bowl, add the flour, cocoa powder, baking powder, baking soda and salt. Mix well.
2. Now, add remaining ingredients and whisk well with an electric beater.
3. Place the mixture evenly into a greased cake pan.
4. Press either "Zone 1" and "Zone 2" and then rotate the knob to select "Air Fry".
5. Set the temperature to 160 degrees C and then set the time for 5 minutes to preheat.
6. After preheating, arrange the pan into the basket.
7. Slide basket into Air Fryer and set the time for 25 minutes.
8. After cooking time is completed, remove the pan from Air Fryer.
9. Set aside to cool.
10. Serve and enjoy!

Serving Suggestions: Serve with chocolate chips on top.
Variation Tip: Refrigerate before serving.
Nutritional Information per Serving:
Calories: 374 | Fat: 22.4g | Sat Fat: 13.3g | Carbohydrates: 39.9g | Fibre: 1.9g | Sugar: 20.5g | Protein: 6.5g

Mini Apple Pies

Preparation Time: 20 minutes | Cooking Time: 35 minutes | Servings: 2

Ingredients:

125g plain flour
½ teaspoon salt
50g shortening
60g butter
80ml cold water

For the Fruit Filling
1 chopped apple
1 tablespoon water
1 teaspoon coarse sugar

Preparation:

1. Trace around a 15cm round baking pan on an 20cm x 27.5cm sheet of paper. Remove the circle and set it aside.
2. Combine the flour and salt in a medium mixing bowl. Cut the shortening and butter into pea-size pieces using a pastry blender.
3. One tablespoon of cold water is sprinkled over a portion of the flour mixture. With a fork, toss the ingredients together.
4. Place the moistened pastry on the bowl's side. Continue with the remaining flour. Form a ball with the flour mixture and knead it gently.
5. Flatten the pastry slightly on a lightly floured board, then roll it out into a 32.5cm circle from the centre to edge. Place the pattern near one of the pastry's edges.
6. Cut a 15cm circle of pastry with a small, sharp knife. Make two circles by repeating the process.
7. Half of the Fruit Filling should be placed on half of the pastry circle, leaving a 35cm border. Using water, wet the naked edge.
8. Fold the pastry's empty half over the filling. To seal the pie, use a fork to press around the edge. With a fork, poke a few holes in the top. Rep with the remaining pastry and filling.
9. Combine the egg and water in a small mixing bowl. Brush the egg wash on the tops of the pies, and then sprinkle with the coarse sugar.
10. Press either "Zone 1" or "Zone 2" and then rotate the knob to select "Air Fryer".
11. Set the temperature to 160 degrees C, and then set the time for 5 minutes to preheat.
12. After preheating, place them into the Air Fryer basket.
13. Slide the basket into the Air Fryer and set the time for 35 minutes.
14. After cooking time is completed, transfer onto serving plates and serve.

Serving Suggestions: Serve with maple syrup on top.
Variation Tip: You can use any fruit.
Nutritional Information per Serving:
Calories: 819 | Fat: 52g | Sat Fat: 2g | Carbohydrates: 73g | Fibre: 2g | Sugar: 2g | Protein: 13g

Homemade Churros

Preparation Time: 10 minutes | Cooking Time: 13 minutes | Servings: 8

Ingredients:

180ml plus 2 tablespoons water
60g butter
1 tablespoon sugar
Pinch of salt
95g flour
2 medium eggs
100g sugar
1 teaspoon cinnamon

Preparation:

1. Bring the water, butter, sugar, and a pinch of salt to a boil in a medium saucepan over medium heat.
2. Reduce the heat to low and quickly stir in the flour with a wooden spatula after the mixture has reached a boil. Stir the mixture continuously until it thickens.
3. Mix everything in a stand mixer bowl.
4. Once the churros dough has cooled slightly, add the eggs one at a time, mixing constantly. Fill a piping bag with the churros mixture.
5. Pipe 7 – 10 cm long churros onto a baking sheet. Using a pair of scissors, cut the end. Freeze the baking sheet for at least 30 minutes.
6. Press your chosen zone - "Zone 1" or "Zone 2" and then rotate the knob to select "Air Fryer".
7. Set the temperature to 180 degrees C, and then set the time for 5 minutes to preheat.
8. After preheating, gently remove the frozen churros from the parchment paper. Then, place them into the air fryer basket of each zone.
9. Slide the baskets into Air Fryer and set the time for 7 minutes.
10. After cooking time is completed, transfer onto serving plates and serve.

Serving Suggestions: Serve with chocolate sauce.
Variation Tip: You can skip the cinnamon.
Nutritional Information per Serving:
Calories: 60 | Fat: 3g | Sat Fat: 1g | Carbohydrates: 8g | Fibre: 1g | Sugar: 5g | Protein: 1g

Dough Dippers with Chocolate Amaretto Sauce

Preparation Time: 25 minutes | Cooking Time: 16 minutes | Servings: 12

Ingredients:

- 455g bread dough, defrosted
- 115g butter, melted
- 200g sugar
- 240g heavy cream
- 300g semi-sweet chocolate chips
- 2 tablespoons Amaretto liqueur

Preparation:

1. Make two 37.5cm logs out of the dough. Each should be cut into 20 segments.
2. Twist the dough halves together 3 to 4 times after cutting each slice.
3. Place the twisted dough on a baking sheet and coat it with melted butter before sprinkling sugar on top.
4. Press your chosen zone - "Zone 1" or "Zone 2" and then rotate the knob to select "Air Fryer".
5. Set the temperature to 175 degrees C, and then set the time for 5 minutes to preheat.
6. After preheating, place into the Air Fryer basket of each zone.
7. Slide the baskets into Air Fryer and set the time for 10 minutes.
8. Make the chocolate amaretto sauce while the dough is cooking. Bring the heavy cream to a boil over medium heat.
9. In a large mixing bowl, add the chocolate chips and pour the hot cream over them. Stir constantly until the chocolate begins to melt.
10. After cooking time is completed, transfer onto serving plates and serve with sauce.

Serving Suggestions: Sprinkle cinnamon on top.
Variation Tip: You can also use almond extract.
Nutritional Information per Serving:
Calories: 419 | Fat: 20g | Sat Fat: 13g | Carbohydrates: 52g | Fibre: 1.6g | Sugar: 34g | Protein: 5g

Raisin and Almond Stuffed Apples

Preparation Time: 15 minutes | Cooking Time: 10 minutes | Servings: 8

Ingredients:

- 8 small firm apples, cored
- 160g golden raisins
- 70g blanched almonds
- 4 tablespoons sugar
- ¼ teaspoon ground cinnamon

Preparation:

1. In a food processor, add raisins, almonds, sugar and cinnamon and pulse until chopped.
2. Carefully stuff each apple with raisin mixture.
3. Line each basket of "Zone 1" and "Zone 2" with parchment paper.
4. Press your chosen zone - "Zone 1" or "Zone 2" and then rotate the knob to select "Air Fry".
5. Set the temperature to 180 degrees C and then set the time for 5 minutes to preheat.
6. After preheating, arrange 4 apples into the basket of each zone.
7. Slide the basket into the Air Fryer and set the time for 10 minutes.
8. After cooking time is completed, remove the apples from Air Fryer.
9. Transfer the apples onto plates and set aside to cool slightly before serving.

Serving Suggestions: Serve with the topping of whipped cream.
Variation Tip: make sure to use firm apples.
Nutritional Information per Serving:
Calories: 261 | Fat: 6.4g | Sat Fat: 0.5g | Carbohydrates: 53.7g | Fibre: 7.6g | Sugar: 40.4g | Protein: 3.7g

Air Fryer Butter Brownies

Preparation Time: 20 minutes | **Cooking Time:** 35 minutes | **Servings:** 2

Ingredients:

60g butter, melted
100g sugar
1 egg
½ teaspoon vanilla extract
40g plain flour
3 tablespoons unsweetened cocoa
⅛ teaspoon baking powder
⅛ teaspoon salt

Preparation:

1. Combine melted butter and sugar in a medium mixing bowl. Mix in the egg and vanilla extract thoroughly.
2. Stir in the dry ingredients until barely mixed.
3. Pour batter into the pans that have been prepared.
4. Press either "Zone 1" or "Zone 2" and then rotate the knob to select "Air Fryer".
5. Set the temperature to 165 degrees C, and then set the time for 5 minutes to preheat.
6. After preheating, place pans into the Air Fryer basket of chosen zone.
7. Slide the basket into the Air Fryer and set the time for 13 minutes.
8. After cooking time is completed, transfer onto serving plates and serve.

Serving Suggestions: Serve with vanilla ice cream.
Variation Tip: You can also add chopped pecans.
Nutritional Information per Serving:
Calories: 520 | Fat: 26g | Sat Fat: 15g | Carbohydrates: 70g | Fibre: 3.3g | Sugar: 50g | Protein: 6g

Baked Citrus Mousse

Preparation Time: 10 minutes | **Cooking Time:** 12 minutes | **Servings:** 4

Ingredients:

200g cream cheese, softened
240g heavy cream
4 tablespoons fresh lime juice
4 tablespoons maple syrup
Pinch of salt

Preparation:

1. For mousse: Press either "Zone 1" or "Zone 2" and then rotate the knob to select "Bake".
2. Set the temperature to 175 degrees C and then set the time for 5 minutes to preheat.
3. In a bowl, add all the ingredients and mix until well combined.
4. Transfer the mixture into 4 ramekins.
5. After preheating, arrange ramekins into the basket.
6. Slide basket into Air Fryer and set the time for 12 minutes.
7. After cooking time is completed, remove the ramekins from Air Fryer.
8. Set the ramekins aside to cool.
9. Refrigerate the ramekins for at least 3 hours before serving.

Serving Suggestions: Serve with the topping of heavy whipping cream.
Variation Tip: You can replace lime with lemon.
Calories: 355 | Fat: 30.9g | Sat Fat: 19.4g | Carbohydrates: 15.9g | Fibre: 0g | Sugar: 12g | Protein: 4.9g

Cheese Apple Pie Rolls

Preparation Time: 15 minutes | Cooking Time: 12 minutes | Servings: 8

Ingredients:

- 330g tart apples, peeled, cored and chopped
- 110g light brown sugar
- 2½ teaspoon ground cinnamon, divided
- 1 teaspoon corn flour
- 8 egg roll wrappers
- 120g cream cheese, softened
- Non-stick cooking spray
- 2 tablespoons sugar

Preparation:

1. In a small bowl, mix together the apples, brown sugar, 1 teaspoon of cinnamon and corn flour.
2. Arrange 1 egg roll wrapper onto a smooth surface.
3. Spread about 1 tablespoon of cream cheese over roll, leaving 2.5cm of edges.
4. Place ⅓ cup of apple mixture over one corner of a wrapper, just below the centre.
5. Fold the bottom corner over filling.
6. With wet fingers, moisten the remaining wrapper edges.
7. Fold side corners toward centre over the filling.
8. Roll egg roll up tightly and with your fingers, press at tip to seal.
9. Repeat with the remaining wrappers, cream cheese and filling.
10. Spray the rolls with cooking spray evenly.
11. Press your chosen zone - "Zone 1" or "Zone 2" and then rotate the knob to select "Air Fry".
12. Set the temperature to 200 degrees C and then set the time for 5 minutes to preheat.
13. After preheating, arrange 4 rolls into the basket of each zone.
14. Slide the basket into the Air Fryer and set the time for 12 minutes.
15. While cooking, flip the rolls once halfway through and spray with the cooking spray.
16. Meanwhile, in a shallow dish, mix together the sugar and remaining cinnamon.
17. After cooking time is completed, remove the rolls from Air Fryer.
18. Coat the rolls with sugar mixture and serve.

Serving Suggestions: Serve with chocolate sauce.
Variation Tip: Use fresh apples.
Nutritional Information per Serving:
Calories: 236 | Fat: 5.7g | Sat Fat: 1.1g | Carbohydrates: 43.4g | Fibre: 3g | Sugar: 20.5g | Protein: 4.5g

Traditional Chocolate Muffins

Preparation Time: 15 minutes | Cooking Time: 15 minutes | Servings: 12

Ingredients:

- 250g plain flour
- 4 tablespoons cocoa powder
- ½ teaspoon baking soda
- 2 teaspoons baking powder
- ½ teaspoon salt
- 240ml coconut milk
- 100g granulated sugar
- 6 tablespoons coconut oil, melted
- 1 teaspoon vanilla extract
- 170g dark chocolate chips
- 60g pistachios, chopped

Preparation:

1. In a bowl, add the flour, cocoa powder, baking powder, baking soda, and salt and mix well.
2. In another bowl, add the coconut milk, sugar, coconut oil and vanilla extract and beat until well combined.
3. Add the flour mixture and mix until just combined.
4. Fold in the chocolate chips and pistachios.
5. Grease 2 (6-cups) silicone muffin tins.
6. Place the mixture into prepared muffin cups about ¾ full.
7. Press your chosen zone - "Zone 1" or "Zone 2" and then rotate the knob to select "Air Fry".
8. Set the temperature to 150 degrees C and then set the time for 5 minutes to preheat.
9. After preheating, arrange 1 muffin tin into the basket of each zone.
10. Slide the basket into the Air Fryer and set the time for 15 minutes.
11. After cooking time is completed, remove the muffin tin from Air Fryer.
12. Place the muffin molds onto a wire rack to cool for about 10 minutes.
13. Carefully invert the muffins onto the wire rack to completely cool before serving.

Serving Suggestions: Serve with the sprinkling of sugar.
Variation Tip: Use best quality cocoa powder.
Nutritional Information per Serving:
Calories: 278 | Fat: 15.9g | Sat Fat: 4.5g | Carbohydrates: 34.1g | Fibre: 4.6g | Sugar: 14.6g | Protein: 4.1g

Delicious Vanilla Soufflé

Preparation Time: 15 minutes | Cooking Time: 23 minutes | Servings: 6

Ingredients:

- 60g butter, softened
- 30g plain flour
- 100g plus 2 tablespoons sugar, divided
- 240ml milk
- 3 teaspoons vanilla extract, divided
- 4 egg yolks
- 5 egg whites
- 1 teaspoon cream of tartar
- 2 tablespoons icing sugar plus extra for dusting

Preparation:

1. In a bowl, add the butter and flour and mix until a smooth paste forms.
2. In a medium pan, mix together 100 g of sugar and milk over medium-low heat and cook for about 3 minutes or until the sugar is dissolved, stirring continuously.
3. Add the flour mixture, whisking continuously and simmer for about 3-4 minutes or until mixture becomes thick.
4. Remove from the heat and stir in 1 teaspoon of vanilla extract.
5. Set aside for about 10 minutes to cool.
6. In a bowl, mix together the egg yolks and 1 teaspoon of vanilla extract.
7. Add the egg yolk mixture into milk mixture and mix until well combined.
8. In another bowl, add the egg whites, cream of tartar, remaining sugar, and vanilla extract and whisk until stiff peaks form.
9. Fold the egg whites mixture into milk mixture.
10. Place the mixture into 6 greased ramekins evenly and with the back of a spoon, smooth the top surface.
11. Press your chosen zone - "Zone 1" or "Zone 2" and then rotate the knob to select "Air Fry".
12. Set the temperature to 165 degrees C and then set the time for 5 minutes to preheat.
13. After preheating, arrange 3 ramekins into the basket of each zone.
14. Slide the basket into the Air Fryer and set the time for 16 minutes.
15. After cooking time is completed, remove the ramekins from Air Fryer.
16. Place the ramekins onto a wire rack to cool slightly.
17. Sprinkle with the icing sugar and serve warm.

Serving Suggestions: Serve with the garnishing of fresh strawberries.
Variation Tip: Use room temperature eggs.
Nutritional Information per Serving:
Calories: 255 | Fat: 11.6g | Sat Fat: 5.1g | Carbohydrates: 31.2g | Fibre: 0.1g | Sugar: 26.4g | Protein: 6.8g

Easy Chocolate Mug Cakes

Preparation Time: 15 minutes | Cooking Time: 17 minutes | Servings: 4

Ingredients:

- 125g flour
- 8 tablespoons sugar
- 1 teaspoon baking powder
- ½ teaspoon baking soda
- ¼ teaspoon salt
- 8 tablespoons milk
- 8 tablespoons applesauce
- 2 tablespoons vegetable oil
- 1 teaspoon vanilla extract
- 8 tablespoons chocolate chips

Preparation:

1. Press either "Zone 1" or "Zone 2" and then rotate the knob to select "Bake".
2. Set the temperature to 190 degrees C and then set the time for 5 minutes to preheat.
3. In a bowl, mix together the flour, sugar, baking soda, baking powder, and salt.
4. Add the milk, applesauce, oil and vanilla extract and mix until well combined.
5. Gently fold in the chocolate chips.
6. Divide the mixture into 4 heatproof mugs.
7. After preheating, arrange 2 mugs into the basket.
8. Slide basket into Air Fryer and set the time for 17 minutes.
9. After cooking time is completed, remove the mugs from Air Fryer.
10. Place the mugs onto a wire rack to cool for about 10 minutes before serving.

Serving Suggestions: Serve with the drizzling of chocolate sauce.
Variation Tip: Use best quality chocolate chips.
Nutritional Information per Serving:
Calories: 409 | Fat: 14g | Sat Fat: 6.1g | Carbohydrates: 66g | Fibre: 2g | Sugar: 39.5g | Protein: 5.9g

Fresh Blueberry Cobbler

Preparation Time: 15 minutes | Cooking Time: 20 minutes | Servings: 12

▶ **Ingredients:**

For Filling:

665g fresh blueberries
400g sugar
2 teaspoons vanilla extract
2 teaspoons plain flour
2 teaspoons fresh lime juice
2 tablespoons butter, melted

For Topping:

440g plain flour
480ml milk
150g sugar
10 tablespoons butter
8 teaspoons baking powder

▶ **Preparation:**

1. In a bowl, add all filling ingredients and mix until well combined.
2. For topping: in another large bowl, mix together the flour, baking powder, and sugar.
3. Add the milk and butter and mix until a crumbly mixture forms.
4. In the bottom of 2 greateaned baking pans, place the blueberry mixture and top with the flour mixture evenly.
5. Press your chosen zone - "Zone 1" or "Zone 2" and then rotate the knob to select "Air Fry".
6. Set the temperature to 160 degrees C and then set the time for 5 minutes to preheat.
7. After preheating, arrange 1 baking pan into the basket of each zone.
8. Slide the basket into the Air Fryer and set the time for 20 minutes.
9. After cooking time is completed, remove the baking pans from Air Fryer.
10. Place the pans of blueberry cobbler onto a wire rack, cool for about 10 minutes before serving.

Serving Suggestions: Serve with the topping of vanilla ice cream.
Variation Tip: Use best quality blueberries.
Nutritional Information per Serving:
Calories: 453 | Fat: 12g | Sat Fat: 7.8g | Carbohydrates: 81.7g | Fibre: 4.2g | Sugar: 49.4g | Protein: 6.1g

Buttered Cherry Crumble

Preparation Time: 15 minutes | Cooking Time: 25 minutes | Servings: 8

▶ **Ingredients:**

2 (350g) cans cherry pie filling
self-rising flour
115g butter, softened
150g plus 2 tablespoons
125g plus 2 tablespoons
caster sugar
Pinch of salt

▶ **Preparation:**

1. In 2 lightly greased baking pans, place the cherry pie filling evenly.
2. In a medium bowl, add the remaining ingredients and mix until a crumbly mixture forms.
3. Spread the mixture over cherry pie filling in each pan evenly.
4. Press your chosen zone - "Zone 1" or "Zone 2" and then rotate the knob to select "Air Fry".
5. Set the temperature to 160 degrees C and then set the time for 5 minutes to preheat.
6. After preheating, arrange 1 baking pan into the basket of each zone.
7. Slide the basket into the Air Fryer and set the time for 25 minutes.
8. After cooking time is completed, remove the baking pans from Air Fryer.
9. Place the baking pan onto a wire rack to cool for about 10 minutes before serving.

Serving Suggestions: Serve with the topping of whipped cream.
Variation Tip: use unsalted butter.
Nutritional Information per Serving:
Calories: 334 | Fat: 11.8g | Sat Fat: 4.5g | Carbohydrates: 55.2g | Fibre: 1.1g | Sugar: 13.8g | Protein: 2.3g

Chapter 7 Dessert Recipes

Plum and Oats Cup

Preparation Time: 15 minutes | Cooking Time: 40 minutes | Servings: 4

Ingredients:

- 495g plums, pitted and sliced
- 100g sugar, divided
- 3 teaspoons cornflour
- 6 tablespoons flour
- ½ teaspoon ground cinnamon
- Pinch of salt
- 3 tablespoons cold butter, chopped
- 6 tablespoons rolled oats

Preparation:

1. In a bowl, place plum slices, 2 teaspoons of sugar and cornflour and toss to coat well.
2. Divide the plum mixture into 4 lightly greased ramekins.
3. In a bowl, mix together the flour, remaining sugar, cinnamon and salt.
4. With a pastry blender, cut in the butter until a crumbly mixture forms.
5. Add the oats and gently stir to combine.
6. Place the oat mixture over plum slices into each ramekin.
7. Press either "Zone 1" or "Zone 2" and then rotate the knob to select "Bake".
8. Set the temperature to 175 degrees C and then set the time for 5 minutes to preheat.
9. After preheating, arrange ramekins into the basket.
10. Slide basket into Air Fryer and set the time for 40 minutes.
11. After cooking time is completed, remove the ramekins from Air Fryer.
12. Place the ramekins onto a wire rack to cool for about 10 minutes before serving.

Serving Suggestions: Serve with the garnishing of extra cinnamon.

Variation Tip: Use fresh plums.

Nutritional Information per Serving:
Calories: 273 | Fat: 9.4g | Sat Fat: 5.6g | Carbohydrates: 47.2g | Fibre: 1.9g | Sugar: 30.4g | Protein: 2.7g

Conclusion

The Ninja Foodi 6-in-1 10-Quart 2-Basket Air Fryer is perfect for air fryer users who want to cook more tasty, crispy meals at once. Its twin baskets are excellent for cooking two different items at once or preparing the same recipe in many batches. It is a multifunctional kitchen tool that can air fry, broil, roast, bake, dehydrate, and reheat leftovers. Although it has all the health advantages of an air fryer, it has the technology to produce food with the same crispiness and tenderness as traditional deep-frying. The Ninja Double Air Fryer also includes useful smart features that make it worthwhile to purchase.

Appendix 1 Air Fryer Cooking Chart

Fish and Seafood	Temp	Time (min)
Calamari (8 oz.)	400 °F	4
Fish Fillet (1-inch, 8 oz.)	400 °F	10
Salmon Fillet (6 oz.)	380 °F	12
Tuna Steak	400 °F	7 to 10
Scallops	400 °F	5 to 7
Shrimp	400 °F	5

Frozen Foods	Temp	Time (min)
Onion Rings (12 oz.)	400 °F	8
Thin French Fries (20 oz.)	400 °F	14
Thick French Fries (17 oz.)	400 °F	18
Pot Sticks (10 oz.)	400 °F	8
Fish Sticks (10 oz.)	400 °F	10
Fish Fillets (½-inch, 10 oz.)	400 °F	14

vegetables	Temp	Time (min)
Asparagus (1-inch slices)	400 °F	5
Beets (sliced)	350 °F	25
Beets (whole)	400 °F	40
Bell Peppers (sliced)	350 °F	13
Broccoli	400 °F	6
Brussels Sprouts (halved)	380 °F	15
Carrots (½-inch slices)	380 °F	15
Cauliflower (florets)	400 °F	12
Eggplant (1½-inch cubes)	400 °F	15
Fennel (quartered)	370 °F	15
Mushrooms (¼-inch slices)	400 °F	5
Onion (pearl)	400 °F	10
Parsnips (½-inch chunks)	380 °F	5
Peppers (1-inch chunks)	400 °F	15
Potatoes (baked, whole)	400 °F	40
Squash (½-inch chunks)	400 °F	12
Tomatoes (cherry)	400 °F	4
Zucchni (½-inch sticks)	400 °F	12
Sweet Potato (whole)	380	30-35
Tomatoes (cherry)	400	5
Zucchini (1/2" sticks)	400	10-12

Meat	Temp	Time (min)
Bacon	400 °F	5 to 7
Beef Eye Round Roast (4 lbs.)	390 °F	50 to 60
Burger (4 oz.)	370 °F	16 to 20
Chicken Breasts, bone-in (1.25 lbs.)	370 °F	25
Chicken Breasts, boneless (4 oz.)	380 °F	12
Chicken Drumsticks (2.5 lbs.)	370 °F	20
Chicken Thighs, bone-in (2 lbs.)	380 °F	22
Chicken Thighs, boneless (1.5 lbs.)	380 °F	18 to 20
Chicken Legs, bone-in (1.75 lbs.)	380 °F	30
Chicken Wings (2 lbs.)	400 °F	12
Flank Steak (1.5 lbs.)	400 °F	12
Game Hen (halved, 2 lbs.)	390 °F	20
Loin (2 lbs.)	360 °F	55
London Broil (2 lbs.)	400 °F	20 to 28
Meatballs (3-inch)	380 °F	10
Rack of Lamb (1.5-2 lbs.)	380 °F	22
Sausages	380 °F	15
Whole Chicken (6.5 lbs.)	360 °F	75

Appendix 2 Recipes Index

A

Air Fried Curry Chicken Drumsticks 60
Air Fried New York Strip Steak 74
Air Fried Salmon Fillets 47
Air Fryer Apples with Cinnamon Oats 14
Air Fryer Butter Brownies 86
Air Fryer Cheese Chicken Wings 26
Air Fryer Red Potato Bites 32
Air Fryer Rice with Peas & Carrots 38
Air Fryer Salmon with Asparagus 49
Avocado Egg Cups 14
Avocado Tacos with Veggie 31

B

Bacon Wrapped Filet Mignon 73
Bacon Wrapped Hot Dogs 75
Bacon Wrapped Pork Tenderloin 81
Bagel Crusted Chicken Strips 63
Baked Balsamic Brussel Sprouts 31
Baked Citrus Mousse 86
Baked Garlicky Mushrooms 34
Baked Parmesan Eggs 18
Baked Pork Chops with Herbs 80
Banana Blueberry Muffins 19
Banana Bread with Walnuts 12
BBQ Baby Back Ribs 79
Beef Mushroom Pastry 22
Beer-Braised Duck Breast 56
Breaded Chicken Cutlets 57
Breaded Mozzarella Sticks 24
Buttered Cherry Crumble 89
Buttered Chicken Breast 58
Buttered Chicken Thighs 67
Buttery Squash slices 34

C

Cheese & Brown Rice Stuffed Tomatoes 30
Cheese & Spinach Stuffed Chicken 69
Cheese Apple Pie Rolls 87
Cheese Beef Taquitos 26
Cheese Chicken Cordon Bleu 69
Cheese Chicken Pockets 59
Cheese Crumb-Topped Sole 42
Cheese Mushroom Rolls 20
Cheese Onion & Green Peppers Stuffed Chicken 61
Cheese Prawn Salad 42
Cheese Spinach Patties 23
Cheese Turkey Croquettes 22
Cheese-Crusted Tuna Patties 45
Cheesy Bacon Stuffed Mushrooms 33
Chicken & Rice Stuffed Peppers 55
Chili Butternut Squash 35
Chocolate Cake 83
Cinnamon Butter Toast 10
Cinnamon French Toast Sticks 13
Cinnamon Lamb Meatballs 77
Classic Hasselback Potatoes 40
Coconut Prawns in Buns 43
Cream Bacon & Spinach Cups 15
Crispy Almond Chicken 61
Crispy and Spicy Catfish 51
Crispy Avocado Fries 28
Crispy Breaded Calamari Rings 23
Crispy Cheese Aubergine 33
Crispy Cheese Garlic Broccoli 37
Crispy Chicken Breasts with Coriander 68
Crispy Courgette Fries 36
Crispy Fried Okra 27
Crispy Herb Potatoes 36
Crispy Oysters 44
Cumin Potato Tacos 28

D

Delicious BBQ Pork Loin 73
Delicious Cajun Flank Steak 77
Delicious Chicken Pesto Stuffed Peppers 59
Delicious Cod Cakes 48
Delicious Vanilla Soufflé 88
Dough Dippers with Chocolate Amaretto Sauce 85

E

Easy Baked Lamb Steaks 78
Easy Balsamic Asparagus 41
Easy Chocolate Mug Cakes 88
Easy Lamb Steak 72
Easy Potato Fries 24
Easy Pretzels Dogs 25
Egg in a Hole 13

F

Fresh Blueberry Cobbler 89
Fresh Kale Chips 29
Fried Chicken with Cheese and Pasta Sauce 60

G

Garlic Butter Bread 21
Garlic Butter Prawns with Parsley 52
Garlic Cheese Asparagus 32
Garlicky Herbed Duck Legs 71
Garlicky Lamb Loin Chops 76
Garlicky Teriyaki Salmon 45
Gingered Coconut Chicken Drumsticks 66

H

Healthy Beans & Veggie Burgers 35
Herbed Beef Roast 79
Herbed Fried Chicken 62
Herbed Lamb Chops 78
Herbed Lime Gingered Turkey Legs 56
Herbed Pork Chops 76
Herbed Salmon with Asparagus 54
Homemade Chicken Tenders 57
Homemade Churros 84
Homemade French Toasts 18
Homemade Soft Pretzels 25
Honey & Mustard Glazed Chicken Drumsticks 66
Honey Glazed Carrots 40
Honey Glazed Tuna Steaks 44
Hot and Spicy Chicken 64

K

Korean-Style Prawn Skewers 46

L

Lemon Garlic Tilapia 50
Lemony Cheese Chicken 63
Lemony Cheesecake 82
Lemony Salmon 48

M

Mini Apple Pies 84

O

Oatmeal Butter Cookies 83
Oreo Muffins 82

P

Paprika Chicken Legs 65
Parmesan Chicken Breasts with Basil 68
Plum and Oats Cup 90
Pork Tenderloin 80
Potato Waffle Fries 27
Prawns in Tacos with Coleslaw 43

R

Raisin and Almond Stuffed Apples 85
Raspberry Puff Pastry 12
Rosemary Lime Turkey Legs 70

S

Salmon Cakes with Mayonnaise 46
Salmon Onion Quiche 16
Sausage & Bacon Omelet with Onion 17
Savory Peppers Soufflé 17
Seasoned Steak 75
Sesame Yoghurt Bagels 16
Simple Baked Bagels 10
Simple Baked Turkey Breast 70
Simple Beef Roast 72
Simple Buttered Green Beans 39
Simple Fried Salmon 52
Simple Hard Boiled Eggs 19
Simple Seasoned Lamb Chops 81
Smoked Spicy Chicken Thighs 67
Sour and Spicy Chicken Legs 65
Spiced Butter Courgette 41
Spiced Chicken Wings 58
Spiced Duck Legs 55
Spicy Beef Skewers 20
Spicy Breakfast Potatoes 15
Spicy Buttered Cauliflower 39
Spicy Cajun Cod Fillets 51
Spicy Cauliflower Poppers 29
Spicy Fried Green Tomatoes 30
Spicy Fried Scallops 53
Spicy Pumpkin Fries 21
Spicy Roasted Whole Chicken 64
Spicy Salmon with Lemon 53
Sweet & Sour Salmon 54
Sweet and Spicy Salmon 49
Sweet Bacon Cinnamon Rolls 11
Sweet BBQ Pork Ribs 74
Sweet Fried Salmon 47
Sweet Potato-Crusted Chicken 62

T

Tasty Breaded Tilapia 50
Tofu in Ginger Orange Sauce 38
Traditional Chocolate Muffins 87

V

Vanilla Cinnamon Rolls 11
Vegetable Stuffed Peppers 37

Printed in Great Britain
by Amazon